Endorsements

I have read dozens of self-help books and followed all their instructions and my life never got better. I never found a book that addressed the effects of abortion and also offered a curriculum for healing. This is what Brick by Brick Healing His Way a Devotional and Journal for Healing a Woman's Heart and its accompanying Workbook offers. It reads as if God is speaking directly to the reader. An intimacy develops between our Creator and the reader so that the burden of pain can be shared. There have been over 60 million abortions since 1973, when it became legal. This translates to 60 million women and an equal amount of men that suffer with the condition of Post Abortion Syndrome. I was one of those women after choosing abortion three times in my life. I pray that these books find themselves in the hands of a wounded person so that they can be free from the prison of guilt and shame. I have also learned that the effects are not limited to the parents but also to the grandparents. I am such a grandparent. As a phone consultant for the Abortion Hotline I met family members – sisters, brothers, cousins, aunts and uncles – that were affected by their family member's choice. The cancer of guilt spreads to everyone who learns about the decision and makes them feel that perhaps they could have done something. We, who have found healing, have a strong desire to help others. I believe that this is evidence of the healing that has taken place. Under the direction of God Himself, Keven Covert was chosen to write these books as her contribution. I admire her obedience and courage to take on such a project and on behalf of those whose healing will be found because these books are available I say Thank You.

Arleen Wong: Post-Abortion, Sexual Integrity and Co-Dependency/Anger Facilitator, Celebrate Recovery Training Coach

BRICK BY BRICK WORKBOOK

*A Journey for Healing the Heart
from Abortion One Brick at a Time*

KEVEN C. COVERT

Co-Authored by Yadeline Franck, Barbara Newton,
Jennifer Perez, Arleen Wong

WESTBOW
PRESS®
A DIVISION OF THOMAS NELSON
& ZONDERVAN

Heart on cover by Steven Da Silvia

WestBow Press books may be ordered through booksellers or by contacting:

WestBow Press
A Division of Thomas Nelson & Zondervan
1663 Liberty Drive
Bloomington, IN 47403
www.westbowpress.com
1 (866) 928-1240

Scripture quotations are taken from the Holy Bible, New International Version®, NIV®. Copyright © 1973, 1978, 1984, 2011 by Biblica, Inc.™ Used by permission of Zondervan. All rights reserved worldwide.

ISBN: 978-1-5127-7841-0 (sc)
ISBN: 978-1-5127-7842-7 (e)

Print information available on the last page.

WestBow Press rev. date: 10/17/2017

Contents

Appendix

⌒ Dedication ⌒

Dedicated to those who have a passion to see men and women who suffer from the wounds of past abortions and loss to be healed, and walk in the freedom the Lord Jesus has waiting for them. Thank you for your transparency and allowing the Lord to use you for His glory. His heart, His ears, and His mouth, together we can be used to see hearts transformed and no longer bound.

Allow the Lord to prepare your heart and guide your passion. You are His chosen, to help hurting hearts begin to live victoriously, just as He has done for you. The Lord Jesus walks this journey with you as He uses you to help transform the hurting to the healed!

❧ Epigraph ❦

I will give you a new heart, and put a new spirit in you; I will remove your heart of stone and give you a heart of flesh.

Ezekiel 36:26

You number my wanderings;
Put my tears into your bottle
Are they not in your book?

Psalm 56:8

The Spirit of the Sovereign Lord is on me,
    because the Lord has anointed me
    to preach good news to the poor.
He has sent me to bind up the brokenhearted,
    to proclaim freedom for the captives
    and release from darkness for the prisoners,
to proclaim the year of the Lord's favor
    and the day of vengeance of our God,
    to comfort all who mourn,
    and provide for those who grieve in Zion-
to bestow on them a crown of beauty
    instead of ashes,
the oil of joy
    instead of mourning,
and a garment of praise
    instead of a spirit of despair.
They will be called oaks of righteousness,
    A planting of the LORD
    for the display of his splendor.

Isaiah 61:1-3

∼ About The Authors ∼

Keven C. Covert is the author of BRICK *BY BRICK Healing His Way a Devotional and Journal for Healing a Woman's Heart*. She has a passion to help women walk in the healing and freedom from their abortions. In 2013, the Lord called her to write a post-abortion healing study for women. This journal and devotional is a healing journey between the Heavenly Father's Heart and the person who has an abortion in their past and desires healing. Since that time, many have told her that this healing devotional is so powerful and full of the Lord's presence, it needed to evolve into a healing study for group healing. Thus, the seed of the workbook/guide was planted. Keven has participated in six Post-Abortion Healing Bible Studies and is trained and facilitates in three of them. She has a Psychology degree and is working on Ministerial Credentials. She was a Pregnancy Care Advocate at the Pregnancy Resource Care Center of Gwinnett. She is involved in the Women and Children's ministry at her church and lives in the North Atlanta, Georgia areas. Keven does speaking engagements and shares hope to hurting hearts which need healing. Keven and her husband Kevin, have three daughters, two son in-laws, and four grandchildren. Her ministry is found on line at www.heartsrestoredandrenewed.com.

Kcovert.heartsrenewed@gmail.com   Twitter: Keven Covert @restoredrenewed   Face Book Page: Hearts Restored and Renewed

Keven's Story

Where does my story begin? My story can begin at age nine when I was exposed to pornographic magazines, thus causing my body image to become distorted because my brain did not know how to process such images at such a young age. My normal and healthy interpretation of what a relationship between two people should be was stolen. Insecurities arose and the need to fill a void was created, yet I did not understand what it was. My story can also begin when I went out on a blind date at sixteen, with someone four years older than me, and at seventeen my innocence was taken from me. I was sexually and emotionally abused for the next eighteen months. When I heard the longtime line, "If you love me you will" I thought that it also meant he loved me. My need to have a boyfriend was so great I stayed with him. After I ended this toxic and damaging relationship, I dated a few guys and had quite a few one night stands. My story also begins when I moved away to get out of the "small town atmosphere" and finish my last two years of college. Once I moved out of South Florida, the Bulimia that started in eleventh grade emerged again. In addition to the binging cycles returned, I started experimenting with drugs and drinking. I was dating guys for purely physical reasons, with no serious commitment on my part. I was waiting for someone in the service to come back and we were going pick to up from there. The crazy thing was, that another side of my personality was also being developed and evident in that I was earning good grades, going to school full time, working two part-time jobs, spending a lot of time at the gym, and being responsible paying my bills. These good qualities were directly related to the blessing that I lived with my grandparents. I know living with them kept me out of trouble, even though I found ways to have fun. My relationship with the Lord was put on hold when I became seventeen; though I still believed and talked to Him. His hand of protection stayed on me.

My story picks up again eighteen months after I moved to North Florida. It was time for midterms and cold weather that Tuesday, the 29th day of February in 1984; it was also Sadie Hawkins Day! While on campus that morning, I met an amazing and incredible guy, whom I had wanted to meet for two months. I ran into him two days later and through some mutual friends of ours, he got the "go ahead" to ask me out. Long story made short, we were always together, and talked about getting married three months into our relationship. It was like God had this whole story planned out.

Everything was going according to plan until nine months into our relationship when I discovered I was pregnant. I had played Russian Roulette for five years, and I thought, "This could not be happening. I got caught!" Immediately my wall of denial went up, and I knew what I was going to do. Sadly, the decision I was getting ready to make had always been in the back of my mind as "my way out" if I became pregnant. I was very naive and knew nothing about abortion. I was a senior in high school when a friend of mine told me she had four of them, no big deal right? The ironic thing is, I had moved in with my boyfriend to see him more. I found out I was pregnant on a Sunday morning before going to church. My boyfriend, soon to be fiancé, wanted to keep the baby. I shook my head no, even after coming home from church. His sister worked in Child Placement at Catholic Charities and his family would have been supportive in all ways possible. I was being selfish and thinking about my family's reputation and name, disappointing parents and shame, getting married in March and graduating in May, and it not a good time. I went through all the emotions we all go through leading up to "the day", even bargaining with God, hoping it was a bad dream. On January 19, 1985, Super Bowl weekend, I had an abortion. My boyfriend drove me. He took care of me afterwards. I had no complications and went on with the wedding plans and graduation. I could emotionally feel the wall of denial building and telling people I had had a procedure done. No one asked questions. Kevin and I got married in March seven weeks later, I graduated in May and a new phase of our story began. Then, on February 14, 2012, the Lord spoke to me to help heal women who have had abortions. Who, me? I knew nothing about an abortion, let alone how to help women help who have had them.

Four months later I found myself in a Post-Abortion Healing Bible Study called "*Forgiven and Set Free*", by Linda Cochrane. All I kept saying for twelve weeks was, "I want my brick wall to come tumbling down". I did not even realize until exactly a year later that the Lord would be using those words and the vision He gave me, my first day of group, for the book He would soon begin to write through me. As the weeks went by, all I wanted was my wall to come down and I remember my passion to help other women grew as the weeks went by. How, I did not know, but the Lord did. I began to co-facilitate "Forgiven and Set Free", and then the Lord placed "*Surrendering the Secret*", by Patricia Layton in my path. Arleen Wong and I started a post-abortion healing study in Ft. Lauderdale in the church I was involved with. I moved two years later and the post-abortion recovery class is still ongoing, touching women's lives and healing hearts. I have participated in "*Paths to Sexual Healing*" by Linda Cochrane, "*The Journey*", by Millie Lace; "Rachel's Vineyard Retreat", founded by Teresa Burke, and "Go Deeper Still", founded by Karen Ellison. I am now a part of the prayer team for Go Deeper Still here in the Atlanta, Georgia area. I volunteer at the Pregnancy Resource Center of Gwinnett, I facilitate *Brick By Brick* healing studies. The Lord continues to use these studies in various areas of my heart.

In 2013, the Lord called me to write *Brick By Brick Healing His Way*. While in my first healing class, I was asked "If your abortion were a wound what would it look like"? My wound looked like the front cover of *Brick By Brick*. It was a vision the Lord gave me that first night of class. Little did I know of the journey the Lord would take me on. In 2013 the Lord called me to write *Brick By Brick Healing His Way*. The Lord instilled in me a passion to help women heal from their abortions at a time when I had yet begun healing myself, and the passion continues to grow. I want to see women be set free of the lies and the chains of bondage the enemy has wrapped around their hearts. I want to see them walk in victory.

My desire is for each one who has experienced an abortion in their life, man or woman, to have the courage to take off the mask they are wearing, be transparent with others and share their story. This is how you begin to walk in freedom, by beginning to expose the darkness of the enemy. Walk this journey with the Lord while He holds your hand each step of the way and He begins to heal your calloused heart, one brick at a time. The Lord will restore your calloused heart and give you a renewed heart. Ezekiel 36:26 says He'll remove the heart of stone and give you a heart of flesh.

A. Loni Wong was treated for depression, fits of rage, nightmares and intimacy disorders for over ten years and not one medical professional told her it was connected to her three abortions. It was in 2005, at the age of fifty, that she began her healing journey. In 2007, she was trained as a facilitator of *"Forgiven and Set Free"*, by Linda Cochrane. From that time to 2015, she would facilitate other Christ centered post abortion recovery studies which included, *"Surrendering the Secret* and *"Concepts of Recovery-The Journey"*. She has also facilitated "Pathway to Sexual Healing", by Linda Cochrane. Keven would meet Arleen in 2012 with a vision of bringing recovery into her church. This message had already been sent to Arleen who immediately recognized this as a divine appointment. In 2013, Arleen retired and began to work fulltime which included serving in a men's prison where she began facilitating, *"A Purpose Driven Life"*, by Rick Warren. She also began working with Keven to establish the first post abortion recovery ministry in her church.

In 2013, she also began to serve as a phone consultant for the International helpline which operates 24/7 for people suffering from Post Abortion Syndrome. Sometimes callers in crisis pregnancies seeking abortion referrals would mistakenly call and she was given an opportunity to be the voice for the unborn. Some changed their minds after speaking with the phone consultants.

In 2016, Arleen decided to step down from Prison Ministry and Hotline to devote all her time to Celebrate Recovery. She completed the 12 Steps in 2014 and now facilitates this same group study. She is part of Calvary Chapel Ft. Lauderdale. She also serves as an Open Share facilitator and Training coach.

Arleen has one son from her first marriage, who has been married to his beautiful wife for eighteen years and they have blessed her with three grandchildren. They live in Broward County.

Loni's Story

I never really recovered from my parent's divorce at the age of two and the abuse sustained from a cruel step-mother, so it was not a surprise when I became pregnant at the age of fourteen. My nineteen year old boyfriend assured me that he knew a woman who would take care of the problem. I was hoping my boyfriend would offer to marry me but that was never mentioned. He took me to a woman who injected Lysol cleaning solution into me. She charged me $25.00. I ended up in the hospital two days later. The doctors were aware of the illegal abortion but simply gave me a D&C and sent me home. One year later I became pregnant by the same boy and the scenario was repeated. Although the first abortion had been hidden from my father, this time he suspected that something was up, and sent me to live with a relative in California. I ended up in the hospital where once again a D&C was performed. I had been treated in two hospitals in two different states and seen by many medical personnel and no one suggested that I seek counseling.

I ran away from home just before my sixteenth birthday and not wanting to become pregnant again, I entered the "Life" of homosexuality. At twenty-one, I became a Playboy Bunny and my first of many affairs with married men began. AT twenty-six I married an abusive alcoholic; had a son and by thirty was divorced and involved once again with a married man. My second husband would ask me to have an abortion so that our "lifestyles" would not be altered. We were very successful as real estate investors, and I did to want to give it up so I agreed. That marriage eventually ended in divorce.

By fifty-three, I had been married three times and my fourth divorce was in my future. It wasn't until I completed a Bible study called Divorce Care that I begin to suspect that these events in my life were connected to something much deeper...somewhere I had never visited. I did not know anything about Post Abortion Syndrome. The guilt and shame burdened me so much that I found it impossible to maintain an intimate relationship. After that first study, the Lord led me to another study "Forgiven and Set Free", by Linda Cochrane. Many years later, Keven would go through the same study which brought us together. Her passion to minister to hurting women was evident and we quickly became an alliance against the shackles of the effects of abortion. God had sent me a message to bring recovery into the church, and it was exactly aligned with Keven's mission. Her book, *Brick By Brick Healing His Way* was published in 2015 and soon the accompanying Workbook will be published as well. I continue to be grateful to God for my healing and to the many that will begin their journey with Keven's books.

While working to establish a post abortion ministry in her church Keven began to write a book. I was privileged to a have a front row seat to witness God writing this book through her. He probably chose me because of my disbelief in the reality of that actually happening to someone. It also confirmed how obedience truly pays off. My eyes saw God's handwriting and His fingerprint on each devotion.

I live a purpose driven life now. I finally have an identity and it has very little to do with who my parents were. I am here to serve God and to help other women who are suffering from the trauma connected with sexual/emotional abuse, same sex attraction and their abortion experience. I pray that abortion ends in my lifetime.

Yadeline Franck participated in the post abortion healing and Bible class called "Surrendering the Secret," by author Pat Layton in 2014. The Lord called her to this Post-Abortion Healing Ministry soon after she began her healing. She is now the Lead Facilitator for *"Surrendering the Secret"* and trains others to co-lead with her at Christian Life Center Church in Fort Lauderdale, Florida. Her passion is that abortion won't be a stigma for women and men but freedom and healing through Christ Jesus. Yadeline is married to a wonderful and supporting husband, and is blessed with two daughters.

Yadeline's Story

Your past never predicts your future. Glory to God. My name is Yadeline Franck, and I had an abortion when I was 18. I grew up in the church and when I found out I was pregnant by the guy I loved, who said he loved me. I thought for sure we could make this work, yet that love would not guarantee that it would not be difficult. Having grown up in the church and my parents being in leadership, I had an image to live up to and a reputation to uphold. I couldn't bear to deal with the fear of what my family would say and the embarrassment and disgrace it would bring to my parents. My boyfriend wasn't mature and responsible which forced me to go somewhere so my secret would be safe. I went to visit my brother and sister-in-law out of state. In talking to them, they were supportive of whatever decision I made. Out of fear and selfishness, I chose abortion. Little did I know how that decision would affect me in years to come.

The Lord brought a very special man in my life who loved me for me, despite my past and all that I experienced. We got married in 2002. Throughout my marriage I have dealt with depression, been suicidal, and tried to figure out where all these mixed emotions were coming from. We have two beautiful daughters and on Saturday mornings they would see their mommy sleep the morning away not spending time with them. Well, that all changed July of 2014. The Lord delivered me from Depression during a revival on a Saturday night at my church and I have been healed ever since! The next morning, my daughters had a mom who got up before them and made the family breakfast. My husband had a new wife full of love and joy. I was full of energy! The days of sleeping Saturdays away were gone! Praise God, those emotions are no longer a part of my life and will never be in my future.

Keven Covert started a Post Abortion Healing class called *"Surrendering the Secret"*, by Pat Layton at the church I attend and I went through the class in summer of 2014. I went through the class for eight weeks and that was a life change for me. Keven also wrote *Brick By Brick Healing His Way a Devotional and Journal for Healing a Woman's Heart,* and published it in 2015. After going through the study and then reading the devotional, I went even further in my healing. While reading Keven's book Jesus healed layers and layers of my past. I am now leading the "Surrendering the Secret" ministry at my church helping other ladies heal from their past abortions. I will soon be facilitating *Brick By Brick* at my church. This is all for God's glory and His grace. I want to thank Mrs. Keven Covert for hearing and obeying God's calling to reach others desperate for a future. Romans 8:28

Barbara Newton is a Nurse and is very active in the Home school community. She has participated in four Post Abortion Healing Bible Studies, and is trained in and facilitates two of them. Her heart is in seeing post-abortive women healed and whole through the grace and love of Jesus Christ. She co-facilitates classes in the post abortion ministry in Ft. Lauderdale, FL, where she and her husband reside with their daughter and two sons.

Barbara's Story

My healing journey from abortion began in 2012, when God placed me with Keven Covert in our first Bible Study of "*Forgiven and Set Free*", by Linda Cochrane. For twenty-two years, I suffered with the guilt, shame, embarrassment, anguish, and regret for my husband's and my decision to end our daughter's life. Plagued with years of depression, suicidal thoughts and addictions, I cried out to God to supply me with a place of healing and restoration, and He more than answered my cry of desperation!

I became a Christian at the age of sixteen, but through the circumstances of the break-up with my fiancé and the development of cancer, I became very angry at God and chose to walk away from Him. My rebelliousness continued for ten years and led me into many dark places and foolish decisions with lasting consequences. The most regrettable was the abortion of our daughter in 1990. However, our God is faithful and what Satan had intended for evil, God turned it all around for good and for His glory and His purposes. God used something so horrible to bring about the salvation of my husband, and my rededication to the Lord, and to further His ministry of post-abortion healing to other women like myself.

Finally, after twenty-two years of seemingly endless pain and anguish, God healed my broken heart and mind through the first Bible study. This spurned in me a passion to let others know there are healing, forgiveness and restoration after abortion. Where was this after my abortion? Why did it take me twenty-two years to be able to find the help that I so desperately wanted and needed? Why do people in the church not know about this and why do they not speak about abortion and recovery from the effects of abortion? For, there are many effects after abortion, but society and the medical community do not want to acknowledge them. The lies of " it is not a baby, it is only a bunch of tissues/ after the abortion, you will be fine/ you will be able to have children after the abortion/ it is a quick and safe procedure/ after it's over, you will go on with your life as though this never happened." These are all lies from the pit of hell, from the lips of Satan, the father of all lies!

It is my prayer and hope that the church as whole, will begin to acknowledge, address and support those women and men who are struggling with abortion in their past. Unfortunately, there is still a stigma attached to the sin of abortion in the church. Post abortive women and men are made to feel as a second class citizen, as if the sin of abortion is not covered by the blood of Jesus. My prayer is for this thinking and attitude to be changed! Jesus died on the cross for ALL sins; it does NOT say in the Bible "Jesus died for all sins except for abortion." NO, His death on the cross covers everything! 45% of women, who have had abortions, have been in the church at the time of their abortion. Do you know how many are sitting in your congregation right now, suffering in silence because they are so scared of being judged, so embarrassed, so full of shame and regret and feeling as if there is no hope for them? I was one of those women. I don't want anyone to have to continue in this type of tortured existence.

There is hope and there is freedom and it is only through Jesus Christ. His blood covers the sin of abortion and knowing the truth will set you free. If this seems like an unreachable dream, it is not; it is real and attainable. Freedom, peace and joy are waiting for you. I will not lie to you; it is hard work, and you will have to visit some hard places, and go back to the pain of the past, but God will be there each step of the way, for He will never leave you, nor forsake you! He was there and continues to be here with each of us, for it is His desire to see you completely healed and restored, as He has a purpose for all of this!

I praise God for His love, mercy and grace poured out upon me, for His refining and shaping me, and to be able to be used by Him, for His purposes, and for His glory! I thank Him so much for all of these lovely ladies that He has brought into my life and for the opportunity to serve Him with them in the development of this workbook to help you receive the healing, joy and encouragement you are seeking. *Brick By Brick* is a unique curriculum for the woman with an abortion in her past. It is a one-on-one walk with Jesus, and a soothing balm to your hurting and broken soul. In this study, God ministers deeply, lovingly, and gently through the author's words which were inspired through God. May God bless you in this endeavor, and remember, He is beside you, walking with you, hand in hand.

Jennifer Perez has a Master's Degree in School Counseling, is a Certified Life Coach, and has graduated from the School of Discipleship Program at Christian Life Center in Fort Lauderdale, Florida. She is active in several ministries at her church, including their Post Abortion Healing Ministry. She is extremely devoted to living out God's will and purpose in her life. Jennifer, her daughter, and her whippet live in the South Florida area.

Jennifer's Story

When I was first given *Brick By Brick Healing His Way Devotional/ Journal*, I remember thinking to myself, "I've had years of therapy and I've already talked so much about the abortions. I don't need to spend all this time doing a devotional on abortion." I prayed to God and heard LOUD AND CLEAR, "You need to do this; you have yet to heal completely from your abortions." I was angry, and I have to admit also scared, upon hearing this from God. Yet, I knew from years of learning the hard way, that when God tells me something so clearly, I had better do it!

As I embarked on this journey, I could not believe how much more there was still to "process"! I was right where God needed me to be to allow the stuffed tears, feelings and blocked memories to rise to the surface.

Brick By Brick's words were so soothing and gentle that it created a very "safe space" for me to face these unresolved issues; as well as a "healing cocoon of warmth" that enabled me to feel safe enough to cut through any remaining denial I had managed to keep at bay.

Brick By Brick's format helped me deal with my emotions in a layer by layer fashion. This was extremely helpful because I needed to do it this slowly. In all honesty, if I had to do it in any other way, I believe it would have been "too overwhelming" and that I would not have completed my healing process. I am convinced that these devotions were written through the Holy Spirit's guidance, as *Brick By Brick* made me feel as if God were holding me in His loving arms as I went through the layers and layers of pain and subsequent healing.

I had experienced four abortions and *Brick By Brick* gave me the room needed to address each one by taking me to the "core" issues surrounding each abortion. Every morning as I did my daily devotion, it created a beautiful quiet time between me and my Savior. I grew to look so forward to it each morning that when it was over, I was very sad and wished that the book had a sequel.

I highly recommend *BBB* to any woman dealing with the issue of abortion, no matter how little or how much has already been "processed." I will forever be grateful for God bringing this book into my life.

Dear Advocate for Life,

Thank you for your courage and obedience to God in stepping out of the boat and into the water to be part of what God is about to do in not only the lives of hurting, women and men, who have suffered an abortion in their past, but in your life as well! This is such a personal and delicate matter, so please do not become discouraged when it seems as though men and women are not coming forward, or those who initially show interest, back out. This is God's ministry and His timing, not ours. After your own healing, you are anxious for the healing of others who were once in our shoes, but He knows the perfect timing for each person's deliverance from this bondage. We are His servants; He will provide the specific people at the appointed time. It is important to have prayer partners praying for you while the group is in session and for you to be praying for each woman and man participating in the study. Satan does not like what we are doing and he will do anything to discourage the facilitators and students in receiving the truth and healing through this study!

Many participants will not have anyone that they can confide in to ask them to be in prayer for them during these next fourteen weeks, so you will be their only source of prayer support. The majority of the women have never told anyone about their abortion, and their intent was to go to their grave not revealing the truth of their past to anyone. This ministry is not for the fainthearted. It will seem draining at times, and we must rely on God to provide us the strength and wisdom to complete this mission He has asked you to participate in. Remember that each person is at a different place: not only in their walk with God, but with their comfort level and ability to share these painful memories. They have suppressed and tried to wipe these memories from their mind. We all have to return to the past- we must feel the pain in order to heal from the pain. We have spent many years running from the pain but we need to confront it head on in order heal. "No pain, no gain."

It is recommend the group size to be no more than six participants in order to help create a closer bond and for time constraints in completing the exercises. This study will be very tech friendly since they will be given the opportunity to complete their assignments on their PC'S. Encourage the participants to keep their phones on vibrate and let them know that they will be used at times during the study. The latest generation is not prone to paper and we want to encourage them to take ownership and become involved. Be ready for many blessings and new relationships the Lord is about to bring into your life.

Please feel free to share the stories we have shared in this workbook. They will be an encouragement of hope to those who are getting ready to begin their healing journey with the Lord. Thank you for going where few will go by helping others to remove the chains of bondage the enemy has around their hearts and to walk in the victory waiting for them.

Love and blessings,

Keven, Arleen, Barbara, Jennifer, Yadeline

~ Inside the Wounded Heart ~

As you may already know, one in three women has had an abortion. When 63% of women who have experienced an abortion live in denial and 73% experience depression it's evident that there is a problem. If 85% experience grief after an abortion, yet have not been able to grieve and mourn the loss of their child, what else do you believe is going on inside of their heart? When 91% experience feelings of shame, unworthiness, anger, rejection feelings of numbness and numerous other symptoms of post abortion, there are too many hearts presently walking around silently crying, and only one hears their cry, our Lord Jesus Christ!

I have found that when I (Keven) speak to a group or am in a setting with many women present, that I do the math and the statistics always catch me off guard to this day. The first thing my heart does is grieve for those women who have had an abortion and are still living behind their wall. Hurt has been built up over the years, shoved down deep and found wearing behind a mask of secrecy. What do one-third of these women have in common? It is the fear of someone finding out what truly lies deep within their heart. These woman share similar symptoms, behavioral changes, personality changes, and life dysfunctions, yet one thing totally separates them. Each of their stories are unique, individual, and have their own twist of circumstances. These ladies who have yet experienced healing from their abortions oftentimes have the same mindset that she is the only one out there that has had an abortion and she doesn't want her secret out. "I'm the only one in this group and I don't want my secret out." The shame she carries is so deep it causes he to go into depression and believes that if she just forgets about it and goes on with her life that these feelings will eventually go away. Her relationships suffer because she feels that if she tells the man in her life or her family of her secret, they won't love her anymore and eave her. The shame makes her feel unworthy of anyone ever loving her. She feels that she is always responsible for the death of any intimate relationship she's in. Ultimately she concludes that she hates men because they are all alike and adopts the philosophy that she will just use them to get back at what happened to her.

These thoughts and many others which are more damaging, go through an unhealed wounded heart. It is our desire to see women's and men's hearts healed of the wounds and trauma from their past abortions. It is yours also or you would not be leading this study. Your heart has begun its healing and will continue to heal as you lead studies. We are all on a journey of healing and allowing the Lords presence to touch our hearts in order to remove the wall of wounds one brick at a time. Thank you for your passion to see others walk in freedom and claim the victory waiting for them.

Healing the Wounded Heart Brick By Brick – Six Steps to Healing

Brick one is for the wounded heart to understand they are not on this journey alone. Their Creator in Heaven is walking with them, and He has their hurts in His hands. The hurting heart needs to believe that God reigns and sits on His throne in Heaven, and that He sent His only Son to die for their sins. They must also believe also that when saved the Holy Spirit dwells in your heart. This step is the foundation for the healing process.

Brick Two is to acknowledge that no matter how well your life is going, every hurt requires healing. We must accept the fact that our hurts created emotional layers very much like building a brick wall. Each row of bricks keeps the hurt hidden that lies behind them. The wall often times becomes so tall and dense that the wounds cannot want to be dealt with. The first row of bricks to take off is denial.

Brick Three is to return to that brick of hurt. This is the most difficult of the steps because it is like seeing a flame and knowing that you have to touch it…just being close to it won't work. It is also like a stone wall that you have built over time, pushing down deep the issues associated with your painful past, yet you need to break through the wall to allow the unhealed pain to be broken and rebuilt in a healthy way. This is where step one is crucial. It is only with the belief that God will walk through this process with you that you will be able to do it. The courage needed to begin to tear down those bricks which have been built over a period of time can only be provided by the Helper that Jesus left us, the Holy Spirit.

Brick Four is breaking through the wall of bricks and one by one picking up the issues relating to your past wounds and working through the pain. This is done by sharing with the nature of your hurt with God and someone you trust. This process can be by journaling the experience and talking to the Lord about it, and then sharing it with that someone. You can also share it with a few others who have experienced your same hurt in a safe place, knowing you will not be judged.

Brick Five is to take ownership of the wall you have built. Be willing to verbally say what the pain in your wounded heart consists of and work on this issue. The deeper you go into the pain and the hurt behind the wall, the deeper the healing that will take place.

Brick Six is to forgive and to receive our identity as offered to us in God's Word. Our identity is no longer based on who we were, what we did or what someone did to us, but instead on who God says we are.

The Heavenly Father's Presence ~ Breaks down the Wall

BRICK BY BRICK Healing His Way a Journey for Healing the Heart from Abortion One Brick at a Time can be used as a study one of three ways. It all depends on how long you want to spend on this journey. Your post abortion healing is an ongoing journey. You may do a quick version or spread it out over a six month period of time or even a full year. This study goes deep into the wounds of the heart as the Heavenly Father's presence is evident in the lives of those hurting. He pours out His loving presence and forgiving grace upon the participant's wound. The Spirit of God moves into the place of hurt and begins to sooth. The ambivalent emotions being experienced for the first time in a long time He sheds light on the root of the heart's trauma. Tears will begin to pour out as cleansing takes place and participants are honest with their emotions. The more honest they are the deeper the healing can be.

This workbook can be divided into a thirteen week study, with the fourteenth week being a Celebration. Each week will have seven devotions to be read and reflected upon. When you have a devotion that has a Part I and Part II, it would be best that the two be read on the same day as one devotional. There will be homework questions to be distributed to the participants. These questions will be labeled for you in the Appendix. This will allow deeper individual study for each person taking the journey of healing. There will be a variety of "Questions for the Heart" to choose from to ask and Healing Heart Exercises to do. You are in control of how many questions to ask and which exercises to perform.

This workbook can be broken down into a seven month study where you meet twice a month, allowing the participant more time to read the devotionals and go deeper into their wound and issues that need healing.

This workbook can also be done in a twelve month study. It consists of meeting once a month, reading a total of seven to nine devotionals, taking a longer time to work on these issues. This can be used for those who are professionals, those in the ministry, and those with families, and full schedules! It allows them to spend more time to reflect and heal, while allowing the Lord more time to touch their heart and work on their specific areas of hurt and issues for healing. They aren't rushed and can take their time. Time heals and in this case it is to everyone's advantage.

One of the most important things I would stress when using Brick By Brick Healing Study, to allow God's Spirit to guide you. Every group you have will be uniquely different. God knows the dynamics that are needed in order for the masks to come off and transparency not to be hindered.

∼ Leader's Preparation for Sessions ∼

Please note, when doing the exercises feel free to change them however you desire, in order to conform to the dynamic of your group. Do follow the workbook in order as to reach every area of healing that needs to be touched. Use creativity to help the healing process go deep, yet remain hopeful and include fun when needed. This study will be very tech friendly, since many participants depend on technology that is always readily available.

You may use websites as a reference for the participants to go to instead of handing out many papers. You may find your own websites for the various topics discussed, please feel free to use them. This saves you time and allows focus on your preparation for your group's needs. You may use your Softcover or EBook, which ever you prefer.

PLEASE REMEMBER: Your first week will be to make sure each participant has a book, and knows what this study will help them do. This is when they introduce themselves to the group. Share the poem "Walk in the Past" before leaders share their stories. If anyone in the group would like to share they can. Give them the Homework for the Heart Week One, found in the Appendix.

1. When you make contact with your participant for the first time before the group begins, do an Intake using the first three devotionals from the study. You can do this over the phone if need be, just so long as you can ask the questions and are able to determine where they are in the process of healing. Read the devotionals to them and ask the questions that follow. It will introduce them to the devotional and give you an idea the level of their brokenness. The Lord will use this time to show you and how open they are to healing. Give them a participant book or have them go on line to order it from Amazon or website Heartsrestoredandrenewed.com. They will have the option of hardback, soft cover, or EBook. Each participant will need a journal to write in. If they use an EBook, answers to the "Reflection Section" of devotional will be written in the journal for that week.

2. Please let the participants know they will need a journal or notebook to write in while they are doing this study. Whether the participant uses a book or EBook a journal or notebook of some fashion is a necessity for deeper healing and participation. Also, the journal will be used during the weekly sessions instead of using handouts. It will cut down on all the papers and allow for more group participation grow and take ownership of their healing.

3. Spend some quiet time or pray before you prepare for your group each week and select which exercises you should do. You will have a variety to choose from. Choose the one that best fits into your group dynamic, and according to how much time allows. Some of them are very intense, others fun. Your exercises will be listed at the beginning of the WEEK including a list of supplies needed. You may construct then the way you feel led!

4. You will need both your *BRICK BY BRICK Devotional/Journal* and workbook. The devotions are not in the workbook so your personal copy of *BBB* devotional will be used as a guide. You will need your book to read the poems before you begin each new section, and as a reference to the individual devotions, since they are not in the Workbook.

5. Each of the WEEKS will have many "Questions for the Heart" to choose from to be used as ice breakers to get the participants sharing. These questions are in the Week's Lesson. You will also have "Healing Heart Exercises", along with the supplies needed for each one. The actual Exercises will be right after "Questions for the Heart" so you have access to full description and can choose according

to your group dynamics. "Homework for the Heart" will also be included in your workbook. You can photocopy the homework questions and hand them out to the participants. You will find the homework exercises in the Appendix. If there are websites to look up for various exercises or information to use for that week's lesson, it will be mentioned for you before the "Questions for the Heart". Websites of their choice can be used as long as website contains correct information needed.

6. You will need to photocopy the "Healing for My Heart" Questions to give each person at the opening of the first week. These questions are in the Appendix. Have the participant answer the questions and put them in an envelope, seal, and put their name it. The leader of the group keeps it until Celebration night. It will show them where they were and where they are in their healing journey weeks later.

7. At your first session, give each participant a carabineer, and explain the meaning behind it. They will bring them to each class and hook them together because they are on this journey together! The carabineer guide will be under the Appendix.

8. There will be homework of some nature for the participants each week. You need to save five minutes at the end of each session to hand out homework questions. Some weeks have more homework questions than others. Emphasize the importance of these exercises. It allows them a richer and deeper healing. Some of the exercises will be on websites they can look up and take notes on themselves. By doing this, they are taking ownership, and you as a leader do not have to copy and give handouts. Keep it simple and paper free as possible. Make copies if it is easier and hand them out to the group.

9. You will need to photocopy "Reflection of the Heart." This is a survey the participants fill out at the last session and return to you. This will give you an idea of the healing they experienced and how much the group meant to them. These questions will be in the Appendix.

10. Each week you will have the "Healing Heart Exercises" that pertain to the devotionals in that week's lesson. These exercises allow the participants to go deeper in their healing.

Overall, this will be a paperless study, and technology will be used whenever possible. You may, of course, give your group something that relates to the topic of discussion or theme throughout the study as the Lord shows you. Be creative and have warm heart moments as you witness the hearts begin to be set free and ultimately change from fear and shame to freedom and joy. Allow the Lord to use you as an instrument in His hands to help hearts walk in victory and be used for God's Glory.

Part I

The Wall Crumbles
One Brick at a time –
Behind the Brick Wall

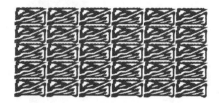

Part 1: The Wall Crumbles One Brick at a Time - Behind the Brick Wall

The first part of *Brick By Brick Healing His Way a Devotional and Journal for Healing a Woman's Heart,* consist of all the issues you can think of that may lie behind someone's reason for not wanting to be healed. It contains all the trauma and memories which they have avoided all this time, not wanting to face the pain hidden deep into their heart. The participants have worn a mask for so long, pretending that life is all good and there is nothing wrong. They are numb to what is at the root of their pain and why they chose abortion in the first place.

You may have women in your group that have never had an abortion, yet they are hurting and grieving due to their miscarriages, stillbirths, ectopic pregnancy, and loss. It does not matter how the loss came about, what matters are the healing of the heart to which it belongs.

In this section you will want the participants to get to a state of comfort to share their story, memories, and testimony. By listening to yours and others they will gain the courage. They will have six weeks to build up enough trust in the group to share what is deep inside. Reassure them that as they share all that is spoken is private and it is not to be discussed outside the group. Every session is confidential.

The first week you meet will be time to share your stories. You may even want to have a guest come who has already gone through healing. Read some of the stories in the Workbook to touch the hearts in your group, reassuring them they are not alone! This will allow participants an opportunity to hear what they can share and to the extent of their comfort level. Once again, remind them the more they share and the deeper they go the more healing takes place. Remind them it will be painful yet fruitful in the end.

⌒ Share from Your Heart ⌒

Opening Week

You can open your meeting with a song to set the atmosphere, light candles, a devotion, or pray. It is your choice. This meeting is an opportunity for the group to get to know one another. Have the women introduce themselves. As an icebreaker ask them, "If your abortion were a wound what would it look like?" Give them some time to answer. They can pass if they are not responding. This will tell you where they are in their comfort level.

This is the meeting to take care of all the housekeeping with your group. These pages are found in the Appendix.

1. Read Group Rules
2. Ask if the group would like to share in bringing snack each week
3. Hand out carabineers and read Carabineer exercise
4. Make sure they have Brick By Brick Devotional
5. Take the BBB Devotional and go over with the group how the devotions are to be divided and read each week. Give them the first weeks devotional titles. Remind the participants to just read those devotions and do not skip ahead. Explain there will be homework for the heart each week. Tell the women to use journals to write in as they go through their healing.
6. Hand out "Healing for My Heart" questions along with an envelope and have the group fill them out and return to you by the end of the group.

Begin Opening Week by reading the poem *Walk in the Past* to prepare them for the next six weeks. From this point on begin to share your story and other leaders with you in the group. Read the stories in the Workbook. The idea is to share with the group how to share on their own.

Each week end with handing out the homework pages.

∽ Walk In The Past ∽

I can't bear to recall the devices which took control of me.
As I replay them in my mind I begin to wonder,
How crazy was I!
Once again, I walk down memory lane of my past.
I can't bear the thought of the screams
And all that took place.
Vivid pictures I see in my mind; yet,
Most of them are reality.
Emotionless and numb at the time,
Feelings being cut off of what was truly happening.

As his little hand reached out
To be touched by my heart, as if to say,
"Let me live, Mommy, I've loved you from the start.
Don't end my life; Jesus has a plan for you and me.
Don't give in to the world's way, it'll work out
Give me a chance, you will see."

I shut the door
Not listening to that still small voice,
I've caved in to the unspoken pressure,
And without the Lord, I have no saving grace.
It is the easy way out,
It won't take but a minute in time;
Yet, little did I realize all the pain
It would bring to my life.

The wall began to grow thick,
While with each year that passed
The memory of my child sank deeper.
Inside, wondering how long this will last.
I never really let go of him,
Though no one ever really knew
The secret that caused me such pain.

Oh Father, help me to walk down my past
And into the pain which lies deep in my being,
All the while knowing You get the Glory
And freedom I gain!
Stirring emotions held deep within,
With life coming out from inside.
My heart begins to open up
No longer hiding behind the pain.
Wall of denial and fear come crashing upon
All along, my Heavenly Father
Has His loving arms around me.

Week One

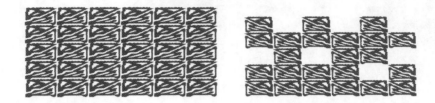

Breaking Down the Bricks: Memories, Past Pain, Father's Love, Inside Pandora's Box, Healing Tears

Devotions from BBB

Questions for the Heart

1. As the Lord revealed the painful memories to you, what went through your mind towards the abuser of your soul? Pg.10

2. What does the mask of numbness you were hiding behind consist of? Pg.12

3. Who or what is at the center and core of your pain? Pg. 12

4. As Jehova-Rapha begins to heal you from deep within, describe what you feel being released from your heart. Pg. 14

5. What do you know about the Names of God and His Character? What does this show you about Who He is? Which one is speaking to you the loudest? Pg.14

6. Do you feel worthy to receive God's love? Why or why not? Pg.16

7. What did you call your earthly father? Pg.16

8.   What is the one memory in Pandora's Box you keep shoving down deeper? Pg.18

9.   Are you willing to pull it out and let all the other pain surrounding it to be set free also? Pg.18

10. Where do you need comfort? Pg.20

11. Because you are continuing to hold on to your sorrow, do you feel closer to or farther away from God? Pg.20

12. At the center of your pain, what feelings do these healing tears want to contain? What feelings are they replacing? Pg.22

13. Name some instances when you have felt the pain of shame or abandonment in your life? Pg.22

14. When you reflect on yourself, what causes you to let down your guard and cry? Pg.22

15. Have you surrendered over your past to God so He can begin to heal you brick by brick, issue by issue? If not, what are you holding on to and why are you holding onto these bricks for security?

Healing the Heart Exercises

1.   Look up websites about the Names of God and talk about them with the group. Have them share which one speaks to them and how it touches them now that they are on this healing journey.

2.   Have each person stand up and repeat: "I am worthy of my Heavenly Father's love". (You may find some cannot stand up and do this. Because of the decision to abort, they do not feel worthy of God's love. I (Keven) had a very difficult time doing this and it was probably one of the deepest healing moments in my entire journey yet.)

3.   Have each person draw in their journals a huge heart on a sheet of paper. Then have them write inside what "bricks" are in there that need to be taken out, one brick at a time. They can draw, label, or otherwise create however they are led.

Supplies

Sheet/pamphlet with Names of God, or bookmarks to hand out with Names of God
Colored pencils,
Markers

NOTES

Week Two

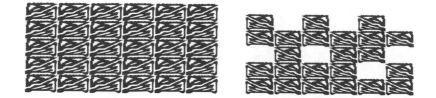

Breaking down bricks of: Fetal Stages of Development, Facts or Fiction, Anniversary Date, What is behind your wall, Tears consist of?

Devotions from BBB

Questions for the Heart

1. Jesus took your pain to the cross. What are you willing to sacrifice for Him so He can begin to collect your tears? Pg.24

2. Who was involved in the decision to abort? Pg.24

3. When your tears fled from your eyes, what emotions pushed them out, and what emotions held them in? pg.24

4. Are you afraid of letting go and receiving comfort? What's holding you back from surrendering? Pg.24

5. How will you gain the courage to connect with the little life that was inside of you? Pg.26

6. Knowing your life has begun to change and your child is in the past, are you willing to begin to reconstruct the wall hiding in your denial? Pg.26

7. Do I truly trust that God knows what He is doing in my life? What signs do I see around my life that shows this? Pg.26

8. How did you feel after reading this devotion? Pg.28

9. Did you receive any counseling prior to your abortion from the clinic or doctor office? Pg.30

10. Has your life continued as normal as they said it would? Pg.30

11. How has your viewpoint changed about the lies you were told since your abortion? Pg.30

12. Have you always lived with emotional numbness surrounding your abortion, or have you suffered with depression? Pg.30

13. What could you do at this time of year to change from a time of depression to celebration? What will it take for you to believe it is possible? Pg.32

14. What feelings are you displacing at your anniversary date of your abortion or time of year your child would have been born? Do others notice them? Pg. 32

15. In reality is it easier to live behind a mask. Why or why not? Pg. 34

16. Have you ever allowed yourself to grieve your child's loss? What did you do? Pg.34

17. What emotions are beginning to surface now that the mask has held you captive is slipping? Pg.34

18. What emotions besides anger and sorrow have I shoved deep inside my heart? Pg.36

19. Where are you emotionally on this journey right now? Pg.36

20. How honest have you been with yourself about all that is stirring inside your heart? Pg.36

21. What kind of questions do you have for the Lord?

Healing Heart Exercises

1. Give out the tears jar to the group and explain the significance of it.

2. Look up websites that have the stages of fetal development and discuss a little to make them aware that this was truly a life.

3. The Mask Exercise: Take turns having each person hold the mask and say what is behind theirs. Then bring out your three colored mask and explain what each color means. The Mask for Healing meaning is in the Appendix.

Supplies Need/Handouts

1. Tear Jars
2. Meaning of Tear Jars in Appendix
3. Masks from Party City, write what you are hiding behind. (3) Purple, black, white

NOTES

Week Three

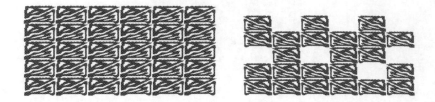

Breaking Down Bricks of Anger, Roots of Pain, Deep Wounds: emphasis is on getting the anger to come out and dealing with in a healthy manner.

Devotions from BBB

Questions for the Heart

1. Are you willing to feel anger? Who taught you it was not safe to feel anger? Pg. 38

2. What are some of the reasons you used to justify your decision to proceed with the abortion? Pg. 38

3. Have you truly opened up your heart and allowed the Lord to begin to heal your heart of the stuffed passion and feelings within? Pg.38

4. Why are you so afraid to fully feel your anger? Pg.40

5. Do you really trust God with this emotion? Pg.40

6. Have you ever thought about how God can still love His children in the midst of disobedience? When you think of His anger, what do you feel and see? Pg. 40

7. Are you aware of the negative tapes in your head? Pg.42

8. At what age did these negative words get spoken into your life and then become internalized and turned into your own self-talk? Pg.42

9. Are you ready to erase the old tapes and create new ones? Pg.42

10. Where can you turn to really find to who you are in Christ? Pg. 42

11. Are you ready to give all my pain over to God? What do you have to lose, gain; or do you still need to hang on to it? Pg.44

12. Who do you need to forgive that caused the deep wounds? Are you willing to let go? Pg. 44

13. Are you willing to share your wound in the group so God can use it to begin to help someone else begin healing? Pg. 44

14. Is there a sense of security you are gaining by shutting off emotionally? Pg.46

15. Do you have the courage to trust God in the healing of your heart? Pg.46

16. What is this false sense of control that you have in your life? Do you actually believe you are in control? Pg.48

17. What are you afraid to let go of and why won't you surrender it to God?

18. Do you feel that if you surrender these memories of pain they will come back, so therefore you feel the need to hold onto them in a safe place? If you let go, would it take you into a painful place? Pg.48

19. Where are you putting your hope? God wants to fill you with joy overflowing; are you allowing Him to do so? Pg.48

20. What was your relationship like with your earthly father? Compare it to that of your Heavenly Father. Was it the same, different or both? Pg.50

21. How do you view your Heavenly Father? Pg.50

22. What traits did your earthly father have that were the same as of your Heavenly Father? Pg. 50

Healing Heart Exercises

1. Carry a bag of rocks around the room three times with your arms out stretched in front of you, shoulder high. Then place them in front of the leader of the group and return to your seat. Leader say's: "How does it feel since you unburdened yourself of the rocks? Can you now place them in God's hands? He is waiting for them."

2. Hold the mirror and speak into the mirror who God says you are.

Supplies Needed/ Handouts

Gallon baggie full of rocks, or stones half full.
Mirror

NOTES

Week Four

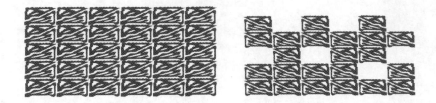

Breaking Down Bricks of: Transparency, Shame, Types of Abuse, Grace for Pain, Surrendering

Devotions

Questions for the Heart

1. As you begin to deal with rejection and how it makes you feel, what other wounds are coming up? Pg.52

2. Who do you feel you have been rejected by and for what reasons? Pg.52

3. What circumstances are wrapped up in your shame so tightly that you won't let it escape? Pg.54

4. Name the people surrounding your abortion that you have anger towards and why. Pg.56

5. In what areas do you show grace to others? Yourself? Pg. 58

6. Is there anyone connected to your abortion whom you are still having difficulty forgiving? Who are they? Pg.58

7. Do you find it difficult to be transparent about your pain, taking ownership of what happened? Pg.60

8. Are you willing to walk in transparency, share the pain from your heart, and help someone else identify with you? Pg.60

9. What strongholds have you struggled with from your past with your abortion(s)? Are you still struggling with addictions to cover up the pain inside that you do not want to deal with? If so, what are they? Pg.60

10. What have you filled your physical body with that covers up what you are emotionally going through? Pg.64

11. What are you doing to comfort yourself which is unhealthy and not honoring God's temple? Pg. 66

12. You at one time may have felt safe when you ate to quiet your emotional pain, yet what were you truly fearful of? Pg.66

Healing Heart Exercises

1. These exercises help deal with the silent feelings that are hidden in the deep wounded heart and deal with those the Lord brings to the surface.

    a. Use a chair and pretend that the person you are angry at is sitting in the chair. Tell them, from your heart, why you are mad.

    b. Use the same chair and this time use a noodle, boxing glove, pillow or anything to release pent up energy. Hit the chair as you vocally express your feelings.

    c. Do both or allow which method is preferred.

2. **This is a must to share concerning question six. Please consider this question due to its nature and importance. This concerns "forgiving yourself" and each participant needs to understand that they cannot forgive themselves; only God can. Here's what you say as the Holy Spirit leads you on this matter.

If your answer is yourself, you need to begin to understand there is only one who can forgive you, and that is Jesus, God's Son. Jesus took your wrongs and your sins to the cross. God sent His One and only Son to die on the cross for the sin of all men. By saying you can't forgive yourself," you are offending God and essentially telling Him the sacrifice of His son was not enough to cover your sin. You are placing yourself above God. Jesus' death covers all your sins.

You cannot forgive yourself alone. Jesus has forgiven you. He wants you to receive forgiveness and accept His sacrifice so He can give you a life with Him in heaven. Allow Him to give you grace daily. Ask God to lay this burden down at His feet at the cross. Leave it down for good and let Him have it once and for all. He is waiting. Forgiveness is a gift for all of us, as we all have sinned. Reach out and accept it and allow the Lord to give you grace daily.

3. Close your eyes to visualize and feel what it would be like for Jesus to be tilling your head and slowly removing the poison from your mind and the lies the enemy has placed within your mind.

4. If you know that there is someone in your group with an eating disorder, now is the time to delicately ask the following questions. It will also be an exercise to be done for homework. Share with them the following. Be led by the Holy Spirit; He'll direct you.

   **What you eat can show the feelings you are trying to deal with and how you process them. Soft foods equates to love, acceptance, comfort, etc... Crunchy and hard foods equate to frustration, anger, anxiety, unexpressed feelings.

   **The binge eating and purging is a vicious, ongoing cycle. When you make up your mind to let go of what's inside causing all this up and down emotional eating and ask the Lord for help, your eating will change. You need to dig deep into your heart and remove the trauma which the eating is covering up. Food may comfort you on the inside, but it does not heal.

Supplies Needed/ Handouts

Pool noodle
Pillow
Boxing gloves
Chair

NOTES

Week Five

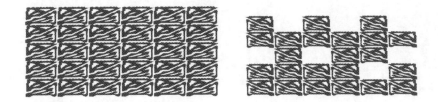

Breaking Down Bricks of: Identity in Christ, Self-Image, Addictions,
Choices of love, Conditional Love and Insecurities

Devotions

Questions for the Heart

1. What are some of the images you have laid down? Pg. 70

2. Can you feel a lightness as you lay down your burdens to the Lord? Do your thoughts become less burdensome as He takes them in exchange for peace and joy? Pg.70

3. Each of us has a God shaped hole that only He can fill. What are you trying to fill that hole with? Examples: food, relationships, sex, promiscuity, drugs, alcohol, your next fix. pg. 74

4. When was the last time you felt joy? Describe it. Pg. 74

5. For whom did you strive to be perfect, and to live a perfect life for? Pg.80

6. What does the real you look like? Pg.80

7. What imperfections from your life did you hide in secret? Pg.80

8. At the time in your life when abortion was done, did you feel abortion was the right choice? Why or why not? Pg. 82

9. If the choice was to your knowledge accurate how do you feel after reading the devotions? Pg.82

10. What devices did you utilize to drown out and stop the pain of your abortion or painful past trauma? Pg.76

Healing Heart Exercises

1. This is for devotional "In My Form part I", an exercise for identity healing.

    a. Have each person take turns holding the mirror up to their face, look into the mirror, and repeat the following after you:

    "I am beautiful; I am loved; I am a daughter of the King; I am God's beloved; I am God's Masterpiece; I am God's beautiful Princess; I am the apple of God's eye; I am God's friend; I am forgiven; and I am loved. I am lovely; beautiful/handsome; wonderfully made. I am the Bride of Christ. I am a new creation in Christ. My heart has been made new. I am set free."

2. Do this exercise as a whole group. Have them respond in their journals individually. Set aside some time to answer these questions. If this were homework, they may not complete it. This concerns the devotional "Defective Choices of Love" on pg. 76 of *Brick By Brick* Devotional. Read the devotion while others meditate on what is being read.

    a. Write down all those who have abused you, hurt you and broken your heart.

    b. Write down the impure thoughts, and lustful desires that you still struggle with and turn them over to God.

    c. What were you searching for but never found in all these relationships?

    d. What behaviors did you engage in to attempt to bring about peace instead of the pain you felt?

    e. What now do you do to have peace in your life?

    After the group is finished writing down their answers in their journals, give them a few minutes to take these things to God and silently pray about them, turning over what they wrote to God.

Supplies Needed/Handouts

Mirror

NOTES

Week Six

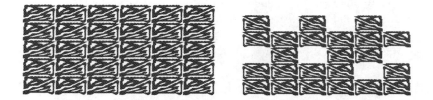

Breaking Down Bricks of:Past Sins and Laying them at Cross, Tainted vs. Pure Love, Facing the Decision You Made, Post Traumatic Stress disorder, Choosing to Share Your Secret with Someone

Devotions

Questions for the Heart

1. What do you need to lay down at the feet of Jesus? Pg.84

2. What emotional scars are present in your life? Pg.84

3. What tapes does the enemy keep playing in your head? Pg.84

4. What memory have you blocked over the years from that "white room experience of innocent violation, which needs to be released into the Father's hands? Pg.88

5. In what ways has God already used the evilness of abortion for His good? Pg.88

6. How will your story be used for God's glory? Pg.88

7. What has God turned from evil into good regarding your abortion experiences? Pg.88

8. After looking at the information for Post Traumatic Stress Disorder, what symptoms do you have as a part of your life, either in the past or the present? Pg.92

9. Are you ready to share your secret with someone? Who will it be? Pg.94

10. If you have already shared it with someone since you have been going through your healing journey, who was it, and how did the transparency feel during and after? Pg.94

11. How did you feel emotionally and physically after exposure? Pg.94

12. As God searches your heart, what will He find that needs surrendering? Pg.94

13. What do you want to give to God and receive in exchange, as in the Great Exchange? Pg.96

14. What are some of the vices you used to escape from your pain instead of running to God? Pg.98

15. Did you ever feel true freedom, or was it short lived until the pain returned? Explain. Pg.98

16. What do you think it would feel like to be totally free? It will happen when you are willing to dig deeper into your healing! Pg.98

Healing Heart Exercises

1. **Very important exercise about our sins Jesus took to the cross.

    Ask question One. "What do you need to lie down at the feet of the cross?" Then have each participant draw a huge cross that they can write inside of in their journals. Have the group then write their sins on their cross. Two:"What emotional scars are present?" Then ask question Three "What tapes does the enemy keep playing in your head from your painful past?" Have the participants take a red marker and cross through the sins written on the cross. Say, "Jesus paid the price for your sins. You no longer need to listen to the lies." Then after everyone has finished with the cross, have them replace the negative with positives, including what Jesus did for them on the cross. Ask them to write next to the cross all that Jesus took to the cross for them and tell what you asked Him to replace it with.

2. Read the devotional on pg. 96, "Great Exchange." Talk about the devotion and what Jesus did on the cross for them. If you feel that there is someone who has yet to receive Jesus as their Savior, please ask them now. In Part II, "Leaning Towards the Cross While Holding His Hand," the very last devotion is the sinner's journey from their abortion. Though this devotion is not in the contents, it is in this journey. It was left out of the book when went to publisher. Maybe this was a divine appointment with the Lord for those reading the devotional who are not saved or do not believe altogether.

3. Use the chair again. Read the Devotion Innocent Violation Part I, p. 88. This time say, "Knowing now that you had a choice to leave the procedure room, looking back, what do you want to say to the one who you feel forced this decision on you? To the one that caused the trauma to begin with? Is it yourself you need to talk to?

4.   **Find a website for Post Traumatic Stress Disorder and talk about the symptoms. Ask the group to share if they would like. Because there is so much to do in this week, choose the exercises that are necessary for your groups healing journey).

5.   Based on the Love Chapter, 1 Corinthian 13 compares Tainted Love and Pure Love. See Appendix

Supplies Needed/Handouts

Chair
Red Markers, red crayons, or red pencils
BBB Devotional on page 88
BBB Devotional on page96
Post Traumatic Stress Disorder Info (use iPad or info you may have already, and have the group look up information on their electronic devices.)
Bible

NOTES

Part II

Leaning Toward the Cross While Holding His Hand
Salvation for the Hurting Heart

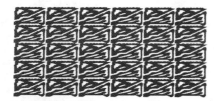 

⌐ Part 2: Leaning Toward the Cross ⌐
While Holding His Hand

Now that the wall has begun to come down and healing has begun to take place, the emphasis is on Who is doing the healing. Some of your participants many not know the Lord Jesus as their Savior. This section leads them to the cross. Up until now, the Heavenly Father, Creator, has tilled the hearts with loving grace, comforted the heart when dealing with the pain, and reassured them of His love for them, and showed them why it is important to confront these issues that have been buried deep down. The Lord now draws the heart to Him. He begins to speak to their spirit man inside and pours upon them a hunger to know His Son. He speaks of Jesus and what He did on the cross for them. These devotionals speak of forgiveness, walking in peace, cleansing, chains being broken, how Jesus saves and forgives by His blood, Jesus is the only answer, and He paid the price for their sins on the cross. They have an opportunity to accept and receive love and forgiveness.

You may have noticed that up until now, the emphasis was mainly on God. It's like that on purpose. This next section leads them to Jesus, their Savior, and their Lord. From here on out you will see the Name of Jesus and Lord more so than God.

*One glitch in the book *BRICK BY BRICK*: the Salvation Devotional on page 146 & 147 titled, I Took It Once and for All, was left out of the contents page during printing. This devotional is in the book and should be read when doing week nine, the last devotion to be read for the second part.

**Begin week seven by reading the poem, Jesus Knows, to prepare them for the Cross. There will be a few questions to ask after reading the poem to prepare the group for what is next!

～ Jesus Knows ～

Jesus was with you in the clinic.
He was with you in the procedure room.
He was there standing next to you as
your child was being taken from within your womb.
Jesus was loving you just the same,
crying for your pain,
'cause He already took your guilt and shame
to the cross that day.
He hung there, my dear child,
giving up His life for you.
Already did He know
the choice you'd make and
what the future held for you.
With Jesus' arms stretched out,
He showed you how much He cared.
He took all your pain and suffering
in hope that your life would be spared.
As He looked out into the crowd that day,
he saw your face among many,
knowing that one day in the future
you would be on your knees, pleading.
Pleading for forgiveness for the mistake you made,
crying out to Abba Father for mercy.
And on His face that day He showed
a deep, passionate look full of loving grace.
The anguish that held your heart captive
since the day you made the choice
to end your child's life
would soon be stripped away empty
and filled with God's love in its place.
So as you get on bended knee
and ask the Lord for forgiveness,
know His loving arms are wrapped around you
as He receives you into His presence.

Week Seven

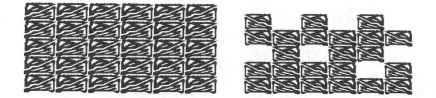

Laying Down the Bricks of Surrendering All Your Sins, Unhealthy Love, Receiving Unconditional Love, Forgiving Others, Guilt, Mad at God

Devotionals

Questions for the Heart

Jesus Knows: Jesus can relate to those of us who have felt abandoned, as many did in, the procedure room. In Matthew 27:46 when Jesus cries out to His Father, "My God, My God, why have you forsaken Me?" We can see that Jesus even felt abandoned and knows and understands our pain.

1. If Jesus overcame 2,000 years ago and defeated our sins, why are we still living in the past?

2. If Jesus stayed in abandonment in hell for three days and then left, taking with Him our victory, gaining the keys of freedom, why do we still have living chains in our past?

3. What is it like to feel the Heavenly Fathers unconditional love? Can you tell a difference your life with His love? Pg.104

4. Compare the type of love you have felt from your earthy father and from your Heavenly Father. Pg. 104

5. What must you forgive your earthly father for before you can trust your Heavenly Father? Pg.104

6. Why are you scared to give God all your heart? Pg.104

7. What does forgiveness look like, and what old images must you replace in your mind? Pg. 106

8. Who from your past do you have the hardest time forgiving? Pg.106

9. What did this person do to cause your pain? Why do you need to forgive them? Pg. 106

10. What runs through your mind when you realize you can't forgive yourself? Pg. 108 Jesus took your sins to the cross for you and wants you to receive Him. He's forgiven you, you when can't forgive yourself. He simply wants you to receive what He did for you by taking away the sin that you have such a hard time letting go of.

11. Will you be able to live a new life without guilt? Pg. 108

12. What do you have to lose by handing over all your unforgiveness to the Lord? What do you stand to gain? Pg. 108

13. Are you mad at God for allowing you to get pregnant? Pg. 110

14. Do you need to put God in the chair and forgive Him? He knows your heart.

15. Do you believe you can let go of the choice you made, and let Jesus take it? In exchange He gives you freedom from guilt and shame. Pg. 110

16. Will you be able to leave the comfort of the darkness and stand in the light of truth? Pg.112

17. Did you know that God is the only one who can forgive you, and, in fact, you cannot forgive yourself? Pg.112

18. What burdens do you want to give to the Lord, and what do you want in exchange? Pg. 114

19. Describe the feeling inside which seems like it is choking the desire to let go of the lies from the enemy. Pg. 116

20. Do you feel worthy to accept the new life God offers you? Remember as you begin to hand over the consequences of your sins, they become easier and your burden becomes lighter. Pg.116

21. As the Lord replaces your misery with His joy and love, my hopelessness with His hope for a future, how does the freedom feel as the bricks are beginning to be dealt with one by one? Pg.118

Healing Heart Exercises

1. Use the chair once again. Have participants take turns putting the person in the chair that needs forgiveness. Have them pretend they are sitting in the chair and speak to them, forgiving them for the pain they caused. If they are having a hard time, ask them what is holding them back from forgiveness. There must be some pain still deep inside they cannot let go of that has them bound. Ask: "What did that person do to cause your pain?" Can you forgive them in your heart the same way Jesus has forgiven you?"

2. Now is a good time to get out the electronics and look up what forgiveness is and is not! Have the participants look it up. There is a list for you in the Appendix.

Supplies Needed

Chair
Forgiveness Is and Is Not (Appendix)

NOTES

Week Eight

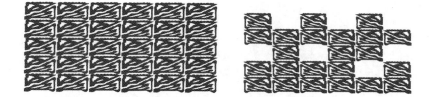

Laying Down Bricks of: Suicide, Anger, Closed Wounds, Deep Pain, Not Loving You, fear, Sorrow, Sins on the Cross, Masks,

Devotions

Questions of the Heart

1. Where have you gone in the past to begin healing? Did it work? Was it a temptation? Where is the only place we can turn to for true healing instead of running and stuffing the past? Pg.120

2. Are you ready for God to give you a heart transplant? What will it take for you to really believe that this is indeed possible? Pg. 120

3. Name the people who have lived inside your closed wounds. How did this affect you? Pg.122

4. What is stopping you from letting go of the burdens that weigh heavy in your heart? Pg. 124

5. What is going on emotionally at the time you may have an anxiety attack? Pg. 124

6. Can you totally let go of the burdens which cause anxiety? Will you be comfortable living with serenity? Pg. 124

7. How will letting go of all life's stressors change who you are? Pg.126

8. Do you believe you deserve to walk in peace? If not, ask the Lord to heal you of unbelief which is a lie. pg. 126

9. What do you believe is the key to building a relationship with the Lord? Pg.128

10. What is one prayer the Lord has answered since you have been on this journey of healing? Do you take all your prayers and petitions to the Lord? Pg.128

   • Philippians 4:6-7 says, "Do not be anxious about anything, but in everything, by prayer and petition, with thanksgiving, present your requests to God. And the peace of God, which transcends all understanding, will guard your hearts and minds in Christ Jesus."

11. Scripture says that mercy endures forever. What has it felt like to receive God's mercy? Pg. 130

12. Can you extend mercy and love to yourself now that you know how loving and merciful God is towards you? You have to love yourself before you can love others. God loves you. Be kind towards your heart and help it heal with God's loving grace. Pg. 130

13. Is there someone in your life that has begged your forgiveness? What is stopping you from forgiving them? Pg.130

14. Who were you rejected by, and where are you in the process of letting go of the hurt they projected into your heart? Pg. 130

15. How does it make you feel knowing that the punishment you deserve has already been served, and you have the liberty to walk away with a new heart? Pg. 130

16. Your testimony has power. Are you ready to share if you have not yet done so? Pg. 132

17. Are you afraid that you will fail once you surrender everything to the Lord, as you have done in the past? Pg. 132

Healing Heart Exercises

This is a listening exercise to help the group hear to the Fathers voice and receive from Him. Read the devotional on page132, My Blood Saves, to prepare the group to talk about the blood of Jesus and the power it has. Ask then to close their eyes and think about the questions being asked to them. Then read the following questions aloud while the group meditates and listen to the Lords voice speak to them.

1. "Take and receive the blood I shed for your pain as truth. Do you believe all that I did for you? Why the hesitation if that is what you are feeling? Your testimony has power and will be used to help others become free of the bondage the enemy has had them in all these years. Are you ready to share?"

2. Afterwards, wait on the Lord, and give everyone a few minutes of silence to hear from the Lord's voice. Then have each person ask the following questions.

   1. How can I remember that the blood you shed, Jesus, cleanses me from all my sins? I realize now that your blood Jesus, even cleanses me from the blood that was shed during my abortion.

* They may get their journals out for this exercise.

* Ask if anyone would like to share their experience.

2. Explain what the tear jars were for and give each person one to keep if you would like.

3. Talk about Post Traumatic Stress Disorder. You will find your list in the Intake Question portion of the Appendix.

4. *This exercise is a follow up from a homework assignment the group had to do in their journals on day six. Ask them, "What color is sin"? Share that sin is not black, it is Crimson/ scarlet red.

    sins are like scarlet, they shall be as white as snow: though they are red as crimson, they shall be like wool."

Supplies Needed

Brick By Brick Devotional, read pg. 132
Tear Jars and meaning behind them (See Appendix)

NOTES

Week Nine

Laying Down Bricks of: What is in Your Tears, Not Trusting God, Identity, Forgiving Others, PTSD, Great Exchange, Grief, Salvation

Devotions

Questions for the Heart

1. What array of emotions did you feel as you handed over your past to the Lord? Pg. 134

2. Did you feel the Loving Water of Healing bubble up in your heart, ready to explode? Describe what you felt? Pg. 134

3. Why are you afraid to cry? Do you feel that once you start you won't stop? Pg. 134

4. Do you feel guilt that you have never truly cried because you feel you may drown in the tears? Pg. 134

5. What feeling overwhelmed you when you surrendered to the spiritual cleansing water which came over you as you humbled yourself before the Lord? Pg. 136

6. Is it your pride that prevents you from acknowledging the humility of Jesus? Pg. 136

7. As the Lord began to crack the calloused shell around your heart, what lies from the enemy came seeping out? Pg. 138

8. Can you trust God to be able to use the memories of your abortion for His glory? Pg.138

9. Do you feel there is someone that you have not forgiven, which is making it impossible to receive my Father in Heaven's forgiveness? Pg.138

10. Where did you learn that grieving was not necessary or should be covered up? Pg.140

11. What runs through your heart knowing that Jesus has your child in His Arms? Pg. 140

12. What part of your mask do you still need to give up and let go? Has it been there for so long it's hard to remove? Pg. 140

13. After taking off the mask, and getting rid of all that is the shadows of your heart from your past, can you imagine what walking in freedom and victory would like? Pg.142

14. What must you do to replace your Heavenly Father with your earthly parents? Pg. 144

Healing Heart Exercises

1. Read Devotion on page 144, "Loving Exchange". Talk to the group about trust, believe, peaceful living, and a heart empty of pain.

2. Sinners Devotion: "I Took It Once and for All." pg.146

3. Read it and ask for those to receive the Lord.

4. Give each person a piece of card stock. Use old magazines and have them make a collage of the "old person" and then on the other side have them create who they are now that healing has taken place, and they have a closer walk with the Lord. The old mask is gone and now the new person is exposed.

Supplies needed

BBB Devotional page 144, "Loving Exchange"
BBB Devotional page 146, "I Took It Once and for All"
Card Stock
Magazines
Glue stick
Scissors
PTSD list, under Appendix with your Intake Questions

NOTES

Part III

Fortress of Security: Walking in Freedom Restored and Renewed Heart

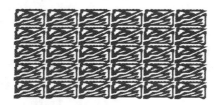 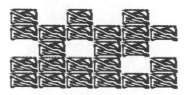

Part 3: Fortress of Security Walking In ‿ Freedom – Restore and Renewed Heart

This last part of the book helps the participant put the wall back together in a healthy manner. By now each member in the group has shared their story; pray that they have fully accepted Jesus as their Savior and are now on their way to walking in freedom. This is when learning how to walk in grace, learning who they are in Christ, and emotional healing takes place, along with unloading any deep secrets they aren't ready to give up, and totally surrendering ALL to Jesus.

The last part is the most rewarding as a leader. You begin to see the transformation of the Father's healing touch upon the individuals in your group. Their countenance changes, they share openly without fear and shame, and they see hope on the horizon. Their journey has been hard in places, but joy comes in the morning.

This is also the part where celebration comes into play. Each person will name their children, memorialize and release giving their child back to the Lord. Remind each person they will see their children in Heaven. Their children are waiting for them and love them. They are forgiven by their Heavenly Father and their child. You also need to ask them what the Lord is leading them to do now. Some participants in the group will be leaders, plant seeds of hope into others lives, or go on about their journey of healing having been made whole, walking down a road of victory.

*Begin Week Ten by reading poem "One by One"

～ **One by One** ～

As I stand in front of the clinic and the tears roll down my face,
I realize now what happened in this place.
The pain I felt then is nothing compared to now within.
The feelings of urgency seemed so important at the time
that I had to end the pregnancy, and little did I understand
what I was truly doing then.
This little life inside would soon be dying and come to an end.
Emotions were turned off; I was totally numb.
I was frozen from fear and the unknown.

As I look back now, twenty-nine years later,
what was I even thinking?
Yet the truth was nowhere in me, or so I thought.
A still, small voice kept calling for me to stop and turn around,
to lay down my fear and trust by putting my knees on the ground.

I couldn't see the light; at the time I was blind,
guided by emotions and what ifs, forgetting the child I carried inside.
The wall of denial began to grow thick, blocking out the still, small voice.

Not wanting to listen to truth and save this child of mine,
I went about my days as though nothing were different,
trying to act normal around others, all the while hurting deep inside.
I had it all under control; my secret was safe, and my life went on as status quo.
I had everyone fooled, or so I thought
until one day I heard the still, small voice once again.
It was the sound of forgiveness longing to be let in.

Week Ten

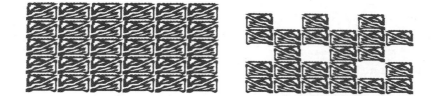

Building A Fortress of: Security with Sharing My Testimony, Courage, Honesty, Peace, Spiritual Warfare, Obedience, Purposeful Living, Grace, My Identity

Devotionals

Questions for the Heart

1. What part of your mask will you share in your testimony? Pg. 154

2. Are you willing to share with women all of the pain you have buried inside, even if it has nothing to do with your abortion? Pg. 154

3. When the enemy comes to tempt you with your past, what are you going to do to stay in the peace of God? What are your actions, not reactions? Pg. 156

4. How has the Lord dealt with you as He has begun to expose your secret? Are you fighting Him anymore? Pg. 156

5. What is your definition of forgiveness? Pg.160

6. Are you ready to begin this new life of walking as a Godly woman/man? Pg. 160

7. What is still lingering from your past that you are dealing with at the moment? Pg. 160 Our healing is an ongoing journey. The more we hand over to the Lord, the more healing takes place.

8. Have you begun to learn how to battle against the enemy of your soul? In what ways has your New Master, Jesus Christ, shown you how to fight Spiritual Battles? Pg. 162

9. What other masters do you need to let go of so that Jesus can take His rightful place? Remember you cannot serve two masters.

10. What has the Lord begun to do in your life in order to have you be more like Him? Pg. 164

11. Is it really a sacrifice to do God's will in your life, or a privilege? Pg.164

12. How has the Lord begun to use your pain for His purpose? Pg.166

13. How is it possible that your abortion is, in fact, part of God's ultimate purpose for your life? Do you see how that decision is being used by God? Pg. 166

Healing Heart Exercises

1. Have the group take a few minutes of silence with the Lord and have them ask the Lord to please use every single traumatic event they have experienced and the Lord has allowed them to go through, to be used for His glory so others may be healed.

2. Give participants the red or white cut out of a heart. Have them write on the heart the names of whom they held responsible for their decision to abort in black. Portion the heart like a piece of pie, and make the piece as large as you see fit and put that person's name in the heart.

3. Now that the hearts have been created, ask each of them to: "Take a moment to look back at what God did for you. He sent His only Son, Jesus Christ, to take the pain of all sins of all humanity! This free gift is for everyone to accept and covers all sins." Have them read the names out loud and voice how they influenced their decision to abort. As you read these names, are there any that you still need to forgive for their part? **Tell them to keep the heart for next week's class.

Supplies Needed

Red paper cut hearts, as large as you can get them
Black markers/pens

NOTES

Week Eleven

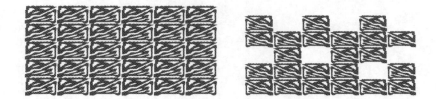

Building a Fortress of: Security with Healing From Sexual and Emotional Trauma, Breaking Soul Ties, Mercy for Others, Victorious Love, Restored Heart, Transparency, Freedom from Past Scars of Verbal Abuse, Loving Yourself

Devotions

Questions of the Heart

1. Are there any memories of sexual trauma or emotional abuse that you have yet to deal with? Pg. 168

2. What has the Lord shown you to do with those whom you need to give mercy to from your past? Pg. 170

3. Do you believe God can really give you the amount of mercy needed to forgive all those involved with my abortion? Ask the Lord to please help you believe that you have all the mercy needed to extend it to them. Pg.170

4. What has it felt like to begin to walk in your healing? How does it feel to become free after all this time of hurt and believing the lies of the enemy? Pg. 172

5. Do you believe that you truly deserve to have an emotionally healthy mind, body, and spirit? Pg. 174

6. What does it feel like when your Heavenly Father lavishes His love into your restored heart? Pg. 174

7. Have you been totally transparent through this study? Why or why not? Pg. 176

8. How can you learn to be completely transparent with the woman or man God has placed in your life to help you continue to heal? What if you are scared? Pg.176

9. Are there any words of verbal abuse and humiliation which need to come out from deep within your heart from the past? Pg.178 Allow God take the hurt and fill you with who you are in Him and as He sees you.

10. What is at the core of your heart that you are so terrified to let yourself see and remember? Pg. 178 Ask the Lord to reveal it as you are ready to handle it.

11. Will you share your mask with the group? Who has been hiding behind it all this time in the midst of pain? If she is a terrified little person, are you ready for the Lord to totally remove the pain and help you heal with His loving touch upon your spirit? Pg. 180

12. Are you ready at the heart level to be transformed? What is holding you back? Pg. 182

13. What is needed to gain courage to be bold for the Lord in sharing your secret so others also may be healed? Pg. 182

Healing Heart Exercises

1. Take the red heart from last week's class and tear up the heart. As each person takes their turn tearing up the heart, have them say verbally "I forgive…"and put the pieces of paper in the trash can.

2. Remind them during this exercise that they cannot forgive themselves. Once God forgives you of your sins, you are forgiven. Saying, "I can't forgive myself," is a form of pride and must be avoided. This places us above God, which is never true. Jesus' blood washes away our sins, not my blood, or your blood, or anyone else. If Jesus forgave us, which He did, we are forgiven, period. Accept His gift!

3. Time to break the soul ties from their past. Have each person write down in their journal the emotional ties and sexual unions they have had in their past (No, not husbands, because some will ask!). Have each take a few minutes with the Lord, give these names to Him, and ask the Lord to break the soul tie from their past. Tell them this must be done to continue with their healing. Explain the importance of breaking soul ties, and how it is done spiritually, and supernaturally as the Lord intervenes. This time is between them and the Lord. Then pray over the group as a whole. Use the devotion "The Father Knows." pg 168

4. Pray over those who share words and curses that hurt. Pray for them to be broken in Jesus' name.

Supplies Needed

Trashcan
Devotional "The Father Knows" pg. 168

NOTES

Week Twelve

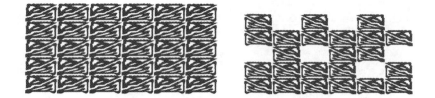

Building a Fortress of Security with God's Strength, A New Beginning, Hope, Blessings, Healed Heart, Anticipation, Fully Surrendered, Forgiveness, Passion for Life, Joy

Devotions

Questions for the Heart

1. If there is still weakness in your heart coming from your past issues that still need healing, would you like to share what they are and see how we can help you heal and work on these issues? Do you fully trust the Lord with these bricks? Pg. 184

2. If you are still hesitant, what fear do you feel is stopping you from being honest with yourself? Jesus has given you liberty. Reach out and claim it and walk in victory. Pg. 186

3. As God has shined His healing light in your life, what can you do to share that light with others who are still hiding behind their wall? Pg. 186

4. What sacrifice are you willing to make for your Savior in order to follow Him until eternity? Pg. 188

5. What daily practice will you establish in your life to ensure that you will continue to walk in this new freedom? Pg. 188

6. Will you let out the passion which has been locked inside from your past, and ask the Lord to bless you for your obedience? How can you begin this process? Pg.190

7. What are some daily habits you can put in your spiritual growth routine so you know that you will be fed spiritually from the Lord? Pg. 190

8. How do you trust in the Lord to put back the pieces of your shattered heart? Will you trust Him that it will be done all in His timing? Pg. 192

9. What kind of barriers from your past have you had to fight along this journey of breaking down your wall and walking out your healing? Pg.194

10. Will you share with the group what you have done to counter act the enemy? Pg. 194

11. Has the Lord shown you your child? Have you asked Him to reveal in a vision or dream who your child is in character, looks and personality? If so, who would like to share what the Lord has shown you? Pg. 196

Healing Heart Exercises

1. Share with the group that this is a journey of healing. The issues they find themselves still dealing with are normal. When they find themselves too weak to do what the Lord has called them to do, they should cry out to Him. He will give them the strength and grace to continue on in their healing process. Many times they feel weak because they are relying on their own strength and not the Lord's.

2. What has it felt like through your healing as the Lord has begun to cleanse you layer by layer, brick by brick, to be set free from your brokenness? Have each person share to the degree their transparency takes them. This sharing alone, as you know, is healing for their spirit.

3. Share with the group how important it is to name your child and memorialize them. Remind them their children are in Heaven waiting for them. They need to be ready. Have them take a few minutes of quiet time and ask the Lord to reveal anything about their child to them. Play a healing song during this time, whichever one the Lord leads you to play. Kari Jobe has amazing songs for healing.

Supplies Needed

Song to be played during Healing Heart Exercise #3

NOTES

Week Thirteen

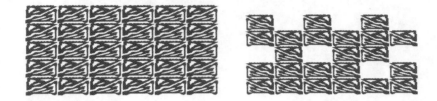

Building a Fortress of Security with Memorialized Children, Releasing Child to the Lord, Firm Foundation, New Mask, Walking in Freedom

Devotions

Questions for the Heart

1. What is keeping you from asking God what your child's name is, if you have yet to do so? Pg. 198

2. As you come to completion of this part of your healing, what new memories has the Lord given you? Pg. 200

3. How are you feeling inside your heart now that you received your child, yet now you have to release them back to the Lord? Pg. 200

4. Have you written a letter to your child yet?

5. Have you written a letter to the Lord yet to say how you are feeling? Are you open to His heart? Pg.202

6. How can you make sure that when you share your testimony you always include the celebration day? Pg. 202

7. As you begin to share your story, think back to what was preventing the first brick to come out of your wall of _____. What was your wall's foundation made of? Pg. 204

8. Do you feel you can keep yourself alert when the Lord wants you to share your story? How can you keep focused to make sure you share what is needed? Pg. 204 Remember, each time you share you may share more than the first time. This is because your healing is increasing and you are becoming more secure with whom you are in Christ. The more you share, the easier it becomes. You are walking in the freedom the Lord has given you and your testimony shows the victory you have in your life!

9. What does your new mask look like? Pg. 206

10. What can you do to turn over all your gifts and talents to be used for God's Kingdom?

Healing Heart Exercises

1. Have the group share what it has been like so far on your healing journey and tearing down the brick wall you built up over time. Did you ever think you would have come this far in your healing? Explain to the group that everyone's journey is different. Due to the nature of their abortion and issues behind their wall, healing will be different for each person. Some have more to process because of the nature of their issues. Our journey is an ongoing process. When Jesus returns to get us or when we go to be with Him first, we will then be totally healed on the other side of Glory. Give God glory and thank Him for the journey He is walking with you, leading you into victory daily!

2. The following exercises are totally up to you. You know the dynamic of the group, who can handle what, and where they are in their healing. Do these following as the Holy Spirit leads you.

    a. Have a baby doll wrapped in a blanket and taking turns, hand it to each participant and give them time to say "goodbye" to their child. Tell them this is their baby. Tell each participant to choose to sing to their child, pray over them, hold them, love them, whatever they desire to do, and give them back to the Lord by placing it back into your arms. Then give the baby doll to the next person. Do this till everyone has had a chance to say goodbye. This was an exercise the Holy Spirit gave me back in 2013. It has been a very powerful exercise of healing with many tears being shed. Play soft music, dim the lights, or do whatever you are led to do.

    b. Releasing the child back to the Lord exercise: Have a balloon to represent each child in the lives of the group. A girl color for girl, boy for boy, a neutral color for those who aren't sure what they have. Take the balloons outside and have the group release them as they let go and let God …

    c. Look up the names of their children and share with them the meanings. There is a book called *The Name Book* by Dorothy Astoria. In this book are the meanings, origins, and spiritual significance of each name.

Supplies Needed

Baby doll wrapped in a blanket
Baby name book
Balloons to represent each baby being released
Music

NOTES

NOTES FOR CELEBRATION

PSALMS 139

1   *O Lord, you have searched me*
    and you know me.

2   *You know when I sit and when I rise;*
    you perceive my thoughts from afar.

3   *You discern my going out and my lying down;*
    you are familiar with all my ways.

4   *Before a word is on my tongue*
    you know it completely, O Lord.

5   *You hem me in – behind and before;*
    you have laid your hand upon me.

6   *Such knowledge is too wonderful for me,*
    too lofty for me to attain.

7   *Where can I go from your Spirit?*
    Where can I flee from your presence?

8   *If I go up to the heavens, you are there;*
    If I make my bed in the depths, you are there.

9   *If I rise on the wings of the dawn,*
    If I settle on the far side of the sea,

10   *even there your hand will guide me,*
    your right hand will hold me fast.

11   *If I say, "Surely the darkness will hide me*
    and the light become night around me,"

12   *even the darkness will not be dark to you;*
    the night will shine like the day,
    for darkness is as light to you.

13   *For you created my inmost being;*
    you knit me together in my mother's womb.

14   *praise you because I am fearfully and wonderfully made;*
    your works are wonderful,
    I know that full well.

15   *My frame was not hidden form you*
    when I was made in the secret place.
    When I was woven together in the depths of the earth,

16   *your eyes saw my unformed body.*
    All the days ordained for me
    were written in your book
    before one of them came to be.

17   *How precious to me are your thoughts, O God!*
      How vast is the sum of them!
18   *Were I to count them,*
      they would outnumber the grains of sand.
      When I awake,
      I am still with you.

19   *If only you would slay the wicked, O God!*
      Away from me, you bloodthirsty men!
20   *They speak of you with evil intent;*
      Your adversaries misuse your name,
21   *Do I not hate those who hate you, O Lord,*
      and abhor those who rise up against you?
22   *I have nothing but hatred for them;*
      I count them my enemies.

23   *Search me, O God, and know my heart;*
      test me and know my anxious thoughts.
24   *See if there is any offensive way in me,*
      and lead me in the way everlasting.

Claim Your Victory

My daughter, I welcome you with open arms on this journey of healing you are about to embark on. It has been a long time waiting and I knew this day would come. It's time to go back to your past so you can be healed and go forward. Sometimes you have to go back, to go forward, and go down a road less traveled to claim your victory waiting for you. This victory is waiting for many women to claim; you are not alone. One in every three women has experienced the same thing you have or made the same decision. Every area of your life is affected by the choice you made or that was made for you. Many women deal with emotional and physiological side effects and concerns which are associated from this experience. The guilt and shame which you hold deep inside your heart and the wall of denial you have built around your emotions will soon be *tumbling down*. The emotional numbness you feel will be opened and that part of your heart will begin to feel once again.

I know this pain you feel deep inside is too difficult to even imagine touching. Whenever the word abortion comes up in conversation your pain of your past is pushed down deeper into the pit of hidden secrecy, yet *I will be holding your hand as you take this journey.* My child, I came to set you free of the bondage your hidden secret has kept you in. Allow Me to take you down a healing road, a rocky one at that, and I will help you make it smooth. The chains of bondage will be broken off. *For I came to set the captives free and it is for freedom you will gain your victory waiting for you.*

The Journey

"So do not fear, for I am with you; Do not be dismayed, for I am your God. I will strengthen you and help you; I will uphold you with my righteous right hand." Isaiah 41:10

Oh My child, how I long to see you totally healed. It will be a process, a journey you will take while I lead, holding your hand. You will not be alone; for I am with you through all the painful memories that you will encounter. *My love is strong enough for you.* Hold on and get ready for the bumps, scrapes, and bruises. Yet, My tender love and mercies will see you thru all that is ahead. Depend on Me and My strength, for without Me you are nothing. It is My Spirit in you that will comfort you in times like these.

Nothing is hidden from Me. *I see all.* I see where you've been, where you are now, and where the road of your healing will take you. There is *victory* at the end of the journey. It is My peace that passes all understanding which will see you through. Let go and let Me be God. Your healing will come in time. The healing process has to begin one stone at a time, one brick at a time, one boulder at a time. Soon the wall of hurt and pain will come tumbling down and I will be here to help you build a new heart which is no longer in the dark; yet, a heart filled with light and My love.

Let Me In

"I will give them an undivided heart and put a new spirit in them; I will remove from them their heart of stone and give them a heart of flesh." Ezekiel 11:19

It is your heart I love My dear child. The mere fact that you are willing to read from a broken state tells Me the condition of your heart. Though your heart is rough and *calloused* on the outside, with dark places you have no desire to go to within, I will *soften those chambers of your heart* and begin to deal with the trauma you experienced. I see your *hardened heart*, I see the deep dark places of pain which you have tried to hide for so long. There is only one thing that can make the pain go away. It is My *forever love and forgiving grace* which flows from My heart into yours. I took your hardened heart to the cross. It was nailed so I could begin to make it brand new.

Allow Me to come into the depths of your pain and revisit each situation with you. Surrender to Me the sexual trauma, abuse, addiction, bondages and insecurities which keep you bound in life. I have the keys to freedom, which the enemy has tried to keep you from finding; and has kept the chains around your heart for all this time. *The bondage and helplessness you feel will be broken in My Son's name Jesus.* He is the One Who has already rescued you when He yielded His Spirit to Me on the cross for you. He is your *Life Savior.* I am your Savior. No one comes to My Father except through Me. When you accept My love I come into your life and *cleanse your heart*, chamber by chamber. Allow My cleansing blood to *enrapture your hardened heart* and begin to make the rough places smooth, the hard places soft, stony places fresh with flesh and no longer hard. The stones have built a wall of denial and escape. The denial which has kept you in bondage all these years, not wanting to face the truth, will come slowly crumbling down as you confront the issues at hand.

The time has come to stop running. Run into the Master's arms and allow *My loving embrace* to comfort the hurt and reach inside, giving you a new heart, a heart which can feel and show true emotion. It will be a heart which no longer hides behind the shadows of the past. I will mend your heart so you can learn to love once again and enjoy what I have longed to bless you with.

Intake Interview Questions for Brick by Brick

1. Have you ever sought out counseling or any type of Spiritual healing after your abortion(s)? IF so, when? (Devotion "Claim your Victory")

2. On a scale of one to ten (one being not at all comfortable/ cannot imagine telling, five being somewhat comfortable in revealing the past; depending on who I am revealing my past to, and ten being completely comfortable with speaking about abortion, and my abortion in particular). Please rate your comfort level now in relation revealing to others the fact that you have had an abortion in your past (Devotion "Claim Your Victory").

3. What areas of your life do you currently feel you need healing in? (Devotion "The Journey")

4. Have you ever or are you currently experiencing any of the following? (Devotion "The Journey")

COMMON SYMPTOMS OF POST-ABORTION DISTRESS: PTSD

Guilt	Self-condemnation
Inability to forgive yourself, let go	Feeling degraded/debased
Emotionally numbing	Feelings of Anger/rage
Feeling s of Shame	Depression
Feelings of Grief and Sorrow	Anxiety
Feelings of Unworthiness	Anguish
Loneliness	Bitterness
Confusion	Fearing God's punishment
Regret/remorse	Hopelessness
Helplessness	Panic
Frustration	Feelings of exploitation
Self-hatred	Despair
Feelings of rejection	Horror
Fear of losing a child	Dreamt of losing a child
Flashbacks	Nightmares
Fear of another pregnancy	Fear of infertility
Feelings of inferiority	Feelings of failure
Being secretive	Sleep disturbances
Crying spells	Division time into before/after abortion
Avoidance of "baby reminders"	Reduced motivation
Loss of normal sources of pleasure	Self-punishing/self-degrading behavior
Developing eating disorders	Alcohol/drug abuse
Suicidal impulses/attempts	Promiscuity/frigidity

Loss of interest in sex

Marital stress

Difficulty with all types of intimacy

Desires for replacement/atonement child

Over-protective of living children

Cutting

Anniversary/ due date reaction

Abusive relationships

Withdrawing from others

Changes in relationships

Damaged mother/child relationships

Failure to bond with subsequent children

Impaired feminine concept

Controlling Behavior

5. How long has it been since your abortion(s)? Devotion:" Let Me In"

6. Number of abortion(s)? Devotion: Let Me In

7. Have you ever experienced any of the following since your abortion(s)? Devotion:" Let Me In"

   a. Dysfunctional relationships
   b. Problems with depression/anxiety
   c. Any suicidal attempts or ideations
   d. Issues with addictions: sexual, food (obesity, anorexia, bulimia), alcohol, drugs

8. Are you totally committed to fourteen weeks of classes to begin digging into your past in order to allow God's healing and being set free from Satan's condemnation of the memories of the abortion(s)? Devotion: "Let Me In"

9. List the people you feel hurt or betrayed by in relationship to your abortion(s) and why Devotion: "Rest Your Soul"

10. Are you able to write down the things you remember about the day of your abortion experience?

11. What feelings, if any, did you experience after the abortion? If you do not recall any feelings or emotions, what was your reaction? Devotion: Rest Your Soul

12. Did you have a relationship with Jesus at the time of your abortion? How about now?

Healing for my Heart Questions

1. Can you describe in words where you need healing?

2. What scares you the most about beginning this study?

3. What do you want to get out of this study?

Reflection of the Heart Survey

1. Something that God did in my heart during this study:

2. The greatest things I'll take from this study:

3. Ways that I believe God wants me to use my story:

4. In order for me to fully allow God to use my story, I need to share my story with these people:

5. Please continue to pray for me about this:

6. Something else I would like to say:

Homework for the Heart: Journaling Exercises

Week One

1. Look up on the computer the Names of God or write in your journal the ones you know. Which ones are your favorites or which new ones jump out to you? Pg.14

2. Picture yourself as a dried up, shriveled root that God is about to pour out His living water on. What are you afraid will begin to grow? Describe what you are feeling. Pg.10

3. What memory of your abortion experience needs to be handed over to God that you need to hold on to, or can't begin to experience? pg.20

4. What bargains did you make during the decision time of your abortion? Pg. 20

Homework for the Heart: Journaling Exercises

WEEK Two

1. Which area of your heart is holding the most resistance? Pg.24

2. What are the tears hiding behind? Are you afraid of letting go and receiving comfort? Pg. 24

3. Why have you been scared to acknowledge there was actually a life inside of you, rather than just a blob of tissue? Pg. 26

4. What secrets are you still hiding from yourself and from God? Ask God to help you surrender all of them to Him. Pg.26

5. How did you feel after reading this devotion? Pg. 28 Devotion "I Formed You". Whatever you can feel, God can heal. Take a few minutes and allow yourself to feel those feelings. Is it difficult? Write in your journal what is going on inside your heart.

6. If you can remember how far along you were when you lost your child, write it down. What feelings are inside your heart and head now? Journal. Pg. 28

7. Do you have a date that sticks out when you think about your abortion? What feelings arise when that time of year comes around? Answer the questions from the first paragraph from this Devotion. Pg. 32

8. Where are you in this journey of healing emotionally when it comes to grieving? Look up on line the stages of grief. Which of the five stages do you identify with right now? Pg. 36

9. What questions do you have for the Lord? Are you being honest with yourself? Pg. 36

Homework for the Heart: Journaling Exercises

WEEK Three

1. Have you ever wanted to tell God, "I'm mad at you for allowing me to get pregnant"? If so, have you yet and why not yet? Pg. 38

2. Are you opening up honestly and being transparent with your heart? Pg.38

3. What are some of the words you carry around buried deep inside? Describe the pain you feel when trying to unbury the past words that wounded your heart. Pg. 42

4. What words do you know to be deep inside your heart which God has spoken to you, which have led to the beginning of your healing? Be open to His goodness towards you. Pg.44

5. Write down the memories the Lord is bringing to the surface. Pg. 44

6. What brick of pain needs to be pushed out first so you can begin to see your wall of pain crumble? Pg. 46

7. As you dig towards the root of your pain and the memories begin to surface, write them down. Don't keep them in. pg. 46

8. Draw in your journal a big heart and section it into four chambers. Label each chamber the following things: memories, trauma/pain, emotions, open. In the center of the heart draw a small circle covering each chamber. Label this root! On the outside of the heart will be all the healing you are doing. Write down your growth and the situations you have overcome and been healed from. Throughout your healing journey fill in the chambers. See how much God is doing in your life as He walks this journey with you. Pg. 46

9. Answer as many questions in paragraph one of this devotion, "Questions of Heart", as you are able to. Pg. 48

10. Do you feel that if you surrender these memories and pain, they will come back to you, so you feel the need to hold on to them in a safe place so they won't escape? If you opened up it would take you into a place too painful to go. Pg. 48

11. Answer as many questions that you can from the Devotion "Father Who Knows Our Sorrows." Pg. 50

Homework for the Heart: Journaling Exercises

WEEK Four

1. What do you feel needs healing the most in your life? What secrets are you still hiding? Pg. 52

2. As you begin to deal with rejection and how it makes you feel, what other feelings or wounds are coming up first that need to be dealt with? Pg.52

3. Visualize Jesus standing before you with His hands out in front of you. Close your eyes and spiritually hand these areas over to Him. Surrender the shame that has held you bound and your heart that has been in bondage to the pain associated with the circumstances. Answer this question: In what area have you seen shame raise its ugly head and are you ready to release it ALL into Jesus' hands? Pg. 54

4. Name the people surrounding your abortion that you have anger towards and why. Pg. 56

5. What has happened over time to your heart due to my holding onto this pain, which has been locked away for so long? Is your heart so calloused you can't begin to open it up and be honest with what is inside? Pg.60

6. What have you covered up your physical body with that covers up what you are emotionally going through? What do you eat when you feel _____? Pg. 64

7. You may have felt safe when you ate to quiet your emotional pain, yet what were you truly fearful of? Pg.66

The binge eating and purging is a vicious ongoing cycle. Not until you make up your mind to let go of what's inside causing all this up and down emotional eating and ask God to help you, will it even begin to stop. It gets to the point where you feel so helpless you don't see the light at the end of the tunnel. The enemy then comes in and discourages you and leaves you hopeless. You need to be aware of this. Call out to God and He'll help you get a handle on what is truly going on deep inside. You don't have an eating problem; you have a fear of feeling pain. Work on the pain and the problem will begin to fade.

Homework for the Heart: Journaling Exercises

WEEK Five

1. Each of us has a Godshaped hole that only God can fill. What are you trying to fill the hole with? Look inside and give God the remaining bricks of denial you still have hidden. Name them and give the bricks to God. There may be pain in the night but joy comes in the morning. Pg. 74

2. Draw a heart in your journal as in previous week. This time call it Heavenly Relief Heart. Inside write what you have been filling that God shaped hole with instead of turning to God for His help. Rather than dealing with issues, the bricks have stayed in your heart. What have you covered them up with what? Pg.76

3. Journal the following: Write down all those who have hurt you, broken your heart, and abused you in your past. Ask God to help you forgive each of them and their sins against you. Pg.76

4. Journal those impure thoughts, lustful and evil desires that you still struggle with and turn them over to God. Write the Lord a prayer, or pray to God. Pg. 76

5. Journal what you were searching for but never found in all these relationships. What behaviors did you engage in, to attempt to bring about peace? What do you do now to have peace in your life? Pg. 76

6. Draw another heart in your journal. Label this Clean Heart. Write inside what our clean heart would have inside, what would life be like when you are healed? What do you hope for? Pg. 78

7. Who do you long to be inside? Pg.80 Take off the mask and let out the real you God created. Who's been hiding behind your mask?

8. What thoughts and feelings did you have with regards to having to put on the mask? Who was the mask for? Pg. 80

9. Name the insecurities which rest inside of your heart. Pg.82

Homework for the Heart: Journaling Exercises

WEEK Six

1. Go deep into your memory and ask God to help you: what memory have you blocked over time since that "white room experience" of innocent violation, which needs to be released into the Father's hands? This way you can look at it from a healed heat and not a hurting heart. Look up 1 Corinthians and compare tainted love to pure love. Pg. 88

2. Look up Post Traumatic Stress Disorder on line: PTSD. What symptoms to you see that you have experienced at any time before you began your healing journey? Pg. 92

Homework for the Heart: Journaling Exercises

WEEK Seven

1. Write a list of all the sins, mistakes and painful events of past which are hidden. Get them in the open and expose them. Then ask the Lord to help you deal with the events which you have yet to heal and let go of. Lay them at the feet of Jesus and give them up. NO longer will they be a part of you. After you have talked to God about them, cross them out with a black pen. Pg. 104

2. So you will be ready for the next class, do the following in your journal: What is between the layers of pain? What does your past have to do with the emotions? What needs to be removed?

   Layers to work on:

   1. Removing past choices
   2. Hardening over time
   3. What is going on now
   4. Locking up bitterness
   5. Liberating present emotion

3. Look up on line and find out what forgiveness is and is not. Write down the differences. Pg. 110

4. Your sin did not begin with your abortion. What was my first sin? Pg. 114

5. Think of someone whom you can share your testimony with that will be non-judgmental and you can trust. Think of someone and prepare to do so soon. Pg. 114

6. What is the first consequence you wanted to hand over for healing of your child?

7. Describe the feeling inside that seems like it is choking the desire to let go of the lies from the enemy? Pg. 116

8. After haven seen the "image of defeat", what changes can I make that will reflect the victory waiting for me? Pg. 118

Homework for the Heart: Journaling Exercises

WEEK Eight

1. Who made you the same offer to rescue you but did not live up to the promise? Pg. 120

2. Are you ready for God to give you a heart transplant? Pg. 120

3. What are you expecting God to do? Pg. 120

4. In the midst of your pain, have you ever thought about ending your life, or were the cuts a warning sign to others you needed help? Did you think about crying out loud, or did you keep the tears silent locked inside your pain? Pg. 122

5. What is the deepest pain inside your heart? Write about it and ask the Lord to help you feel all the feelings surrounding the issue. Believe this to be possible. Pg. 122

6. Do you truly trust the Lord to walk this journey of healing with you, hold your hand, and show you the way to heal? Your security is in God. What have you been putting your security in? pg. 126

7. There may be scars left in your heart from rejection. What is the rejection from? Can you talk about it? If so, do write in your journal to help get them out so you can face the scars once and for all. Pg. 130

8. What sins are hard to face and admit? Are you ready to let go of the past? Pg. 130

9. Take and receive the blood Jesus shed for your pain as truth. Do you believe all that He did for you? Why the hesitation if that is what you are feeling? Pg. 132

10. Your testimony has power. Are you ready to share your secret? Pg. 132

11. Ask yourself: How can I remember the blood Jesus shed, and that He cleansed me from all my sins, and that His blood cleanses me from the blood that was shed during my abortion? Pg. 132

12. Draw a large picture of a cross in your journal. Write down what color sin is. You will need this for your next meeting

13. Memorize Philippians 4: 6-7. Write it down in your journal.

Homework for the Heart: Journaling Exercises

WEEK Nine

1. Journal: Why are you afraid to start cry? Is it once you start you won't stop? Do you feel guilty that you have never truly cried because you're afraid the tears will be so many, it will feel like you are drowning? Pg. 136

2. How can you be sure that you are handing everything over to God? What if there is still some pain left and some bricks that have not even been touched? Pg. 136

3. Can you trust God to be able to use the memories of your abortion for His glory? Pg. 140

4. What has been in the shadows all this time covered by chains of shame from the enemy, yet has been broken by Christ's love for you? Pg. 142

5. Have you lived in your state of torment and dread, depression, guilt, and shame for so long, that you have no idea what it would be like to live in victory? Pg. 142 Imagine the chains around your heart are off and your heart is no longer calloused. What would it feel like to walk around in that kind of freedom? Share it in your journal and then in class.

6. Write a letter to another woman who has an abortion in her past. What would God say to her? Pg. 142

7. How can the Lord use your pain and testimony to touch other's lives? Do you see the freedom from each can be used for the good? Pg. 144

8. Am I ready for God to exchange my past trauma for an abundance of love, joy, peace, forgiveness, faith, and courage? Pg. 144

9. Read the letter out loud you wrote yesterday. This is God's letter to you. You are a daughter of the King. He loves you and has grace for you. Pg. 144

10. What is the first step you can take in your life that will reflect the forgiveness you have received? Pg. 146

11. Are you willing to share the events surrounding your abortion so that others may find their healing? Pg. 146

12. **I Took It Once and For All (pg. 146) Prayer**

Are you still saying, "I know God forgives me, but I can't forgive myself"? If those are your words, look and listen to what you are really saying to God. This is a hard one, but hearing it said to me (Barbara) was what I needed to finally,once and for all, accept God's forgiveness for the abortion and to finally stop beating myself up. You can't forgive yourself. When you do say "I can't forgive myself," you are ultimately telling God that the sacrifice of Jesus, His Son, was NOT enough! Jesus' death on the cross was NOT enough to cover your sin. You know that is NOT the truth. Jesus' sacrifice of death WAS ENOUGH to cover your and my sin of abortion!

The truth of the matter is you can't forgive yourself. You have to give your sin of abortion to Jesus and accept His ultimate gift of forgiveness for your sins. Accept His forgiveness because He paid your punishment for you.

I accept what Jesus did for me because Jesus forgives and loves me!!

Homework for the Heart: Journaling Exercises

WEEK Ten

1. It is time to write a letter to your child (ren). Begin to think about what you would like to tell them.

2. Do I have the courage necessary to let go of the familiar and step into the unfamiliar? Ask the Lord to help you remember that stepping into the unknown is exactly the place where you will find Him. Pg. 158

3. Is there anything else you need to turn over to the Lord? You may not know what it is, yet you can describe the feeling that something else needs to come out, even if you do not know what it is. Pg. 160 Remember, this journey is ongoing. The Lord may reveal something to you when you least expect it. It is very normal occurrence for people who have gone through healing.

4. Write a letter of encouragement to another post abortive woman/man. Talk about your healing journey, what Jesus has done in your life, and how they can experience this life change also. Pg. 162

Homework for the Heart: Journaling Exercises

WEEK Eleven

1. What has it felt like to begin to walk in your healing and freedom from your past? Pg. 172

2. What does it feel like to receive the unconditional and victorious love from your Heavenly Father, when all you received while growing up was conditional love? Pg. 172

3. Your heart has been restored and is now being lavished with the Heavenly Father's love for you. What does your heart feel like now compared to before you started this journey? Pg. 174

4. Journal about the words that were spoken over you and who spoke them. Turn them over to the Lord and ask Him in prayer to remove the old tapes and for you to see who you are in Him, who He knows you to be. Pg. 178

5. Look up on line some Scriptures that talk about Who am I in Christ, and your identity in Christ. Write down the ones that speak to you and repeat them over yourself each day. Pg. 178

6. Ask the Lord to help you remove the mask you have been hiding behind and help you to put on a new one. Pg. 180 If you are scared, and there are issues you can't yet face due to the depth of the pain associate with it, it will come out in due time. God knows what you can handle and will bring the issues out in due time and heal that part of you.

7. Ask the Lord who you should share your secret with. Who is safe to tell? Pg. 182

Homework for the Heart: Journaling Exercises

WEEK Twelve

1. Look up on line scriptures that have to do with children in heaven. Write them down in your journal. Pg. 196

2. Ask the Lord to reveal your child (ran)'s name and sex to you.

3. Write them a poem, song, draw or paint a picture, plant a rose bush or tree. Buy something that reminds you of them that the Lord has shared with you. Be creative, and have it be from your heart to your child's heart. Bring it to share with the group if you'd like. It is very important in the grieving process to have something as a positive reminder/memorial of your children. It helps bring closure, along with the reassurance that we will one day be reunited with them.

Homework for the Heart: Journaling Exercises

WEEK 13

1. How do you release your child back over to the Lord, when you feel like you have just received them? Pg. 200

2. Write a letter to the Lord and tell Him thank you for your healing and how you feel with a newly restored and renewed heart. Pg. 200

3. This is a day of celebration/release: celebration for all that God has done for you and in you these last several weeks, and a day to release – our children back to God, without the previous shackles which entwined us. There is a time for grief and a time for rejoicing. For everything under the sun there is a time. Pg. 202

4. Make a list of ways you can shine the light of Jesus into other's lives. Pg. 206

5. What is the Lord speaking to your heart to do now with your healing?

∽ Group Rules ∽

1. Confidentiality is to be maintained at all times.

2. Commitment to working through the whole study by doing all assignments is needed.

3. You must attend all meetings – no more than two absence's.

4. You have the freedom to exit the room if you needed.

5. Each member will be expected to participate, as this helps the healing process.

6. Please do not rescue a neighbor, meaning, for example, no handing a tissue for tears or a hug for comfort. Allow the Lord to be the one to comfort.

7. No feedback from anyone in the group can be judging or condemning.

8. Do not give advice.

9. Do not monopolize; allow others to share so they may receive healing.

10. No cross talking; conversation should pertain to study.

11. Be faithful to be here on time, and contact your leader if you are running late via text.

12. Please put your cell phones on silent. Bring them out only when needed for study. Be respectful to others in the group concerning use of phone.

⌒ The Story behind CARABINERS ⌒

Think of the next fourteen weeks as learning how to break through a brick wall, taking one brick out at a time and rebuilding into a secure fortress. As this wall stares you in the face and you try to figure out how to begin to destroy it, others will be with you doing the same thing. Over this course of time, you will be searching your heart and going back to your past to figure out how to move ahead to your healing. It won't be easy; it will be painful at times, yet worth every moment of hard work. You will also be learning techniques from each other as a group, and listening to plans from the Master Builder! He will show you how to confront the fear and pain one brick at a time. You will become construction workers and watch the Master Builder show you the best way to have your wall come crumbling down and rebuild it into a strong fortress in Him. The teamwork strengthens our spirits and brings us closer to each other and to God.

Tackling this wall will take faith and courage. There is no way to go around it. We don't have the strength to destroy it by ourselves. As a group, we are going together. We will face together what makes up this wall – every aspect of each others' abortion experience. Week by week we will deal with more bricks, and more issues that need to be healed from our past. We will journey this road together. We will see the Master Builder lead the way, and He will begin to knock down this wall for us.

Our calloused hearts will have their shells broken, and the soil will be tilled. Out of our broken hearts will come new life, ready to walk in freedom. We each have victory waiting on the other side of this brick wall. We will succeed in establishing a strong fortress and a victorious result.

A carabineer is a tool that mountain climbers use to assist them as they climb. Carabineers are linked to one another, making climbers stronger for the journey and helping them stay together. The carabineer is going to represent our plans to turn our wall into a fortress.

1. It connects us to the One who leads the group and Who anchored us.

2. It reminds us that we must remain clipped together.

3. It is evidence of our desire to be set free

4. It should prompt us to read a Scripture when we see it.

5. What the enemy wants is for you to unclip yourself from the group.

So put your carabineer where you will see it; attach it to your key chain, for instance, and be sure to bring it with you each week!

⌒ **Five Stages of Grief** ⌒

First Stage is Denial:

Denial is a conscious or unconscious refusal to accept facts, information, or reality, relating to a situation. It is a defense mechanism and is perfectly natural. Some people can become locked in this stage when dealing with a traumatic change that can be ignored. Death, of course, is not particularly easy to avoid indefinitely.

A wall of denial is the hardest to break through. This wall began construction during their abortion experience, before or after pregnancy. The wall has been established since the moment of conception. Their emotions began to turn off so the pain of having to make a decision would be easier. Many go through life totally numb to the experience, turning off their emotions altogether. Eventually the denial will be too heavy to bear, and it is the first of the layers to be healed.

Second Stage is Anger:

Anger can manifest in different ways. People dealing with emotional upset can be angry with themselves, and or with others, especially those close to them. Knowing this helps you remain detached and non-judgmental when experiencing the anger of someone who is very upset.

A person who has experienced an abortion has stored up anger, that has been repressed over a period of time. They will become angry for reasons that are minor and go overboard in expressing this emotion. They know they are angry, yet are unaware of the underlying reason. If someone has neglect of any nature in their background and stuffs it deep inside, piling more loss on top of it, they will explode eventually. The circumstance behind the trauma needs to be dealt with and healed in order to live life in a healthy way. Get to the root of the anger and deal with it no matter how painful it will be.

Third Stage is Bargaining

This happens when people face death or a very traumatic circumstance. They begin to bargain with whatever God the person believes in. People facing less serious trauma can bargain or seek to negotiate a compromise. It rarely provides a sustainable solution, especially in life or death.

People who find themselves pregnant often do the same thing. They start to ask for it to be taken away and almost pretend it isn't happening. The denial gets in the way, and eventually it overtakes them. The bargaining is not working, which leads to the next stage.

Fourth Stage is Depression

It is natural to feel sadness, regret, fear, uncertainty, and other similar emotions when a major loss occurs in your life. It shows that the person has at least begun to accept the reality that something is gone for good. Deep depression is taking the emotional attachment the person's loss is associated with, and not being able to see reality. It is refusal to accept this person is gone and inability to accept the loss.

When someone chooses abortion and is emotionally dealing with the decision of whether it was right or wrong, emotions of regret surface to the extreme. Many people stay in this stage and cannot cope with reality around them. Some go through life appearing normal and healthy, yet deep inside they are in such deep pain it is hard to function normally. Their remorse and regret for the decision they made is still very much a part of their everyday life. Healing is needed to deal with the situation of their abortion as a whole. The Lord Himself comes to the hurting heart and begins to heal it of these emotions.

Fifth Stage is Acceptance

This stage definitely varies according to the person's situation, although broadly it is an indication there is some emotional detachment and objectivity. People dying can enter this stage a long time before the people they leave behind. Acceptance of reality is accomplished in this stage.

To a person who finally accepts that the choice they made was to have an abortion, this is truly one of the most difficult and emotional of all five stages. To verbally say, "I aborted my child," is very difficult for anyone. The emotional impact is beyond words, and over a period of time, the acceptance of the choice that was made becomes easier to handle and face.

I (Keven) had the most difficult time with this stage. Not until after *Brick By Brick Healing His Way Devotional/ Journal* was written and published did I go through this stage. It was at a healing retreat. It impacted me so much in my spirit. Once I said the words, reality set in and the most significant healing took place yet. God's grace was upon me and strengthened me. I (Keven) cried the hardest, with the most tears that I have cried yet in my healing. My healing began in 2012, and this retreat was in September 2015, four years later.

Bottom line is that each person needs to go through the five stages of grief. Some will fly right through them, while others will spend more time in a particular stage of grief. Reassure each person this is possible to get through, and by going through the pain and tears, they can live a healthy functioning life that the Lord has waiting for them.

⤳ Why Tear Bottles ⤳

Psalm 56:8 says, "Record my lament; list my tears on your scrolls, are they not in your record." Other versions use the word bottles instead of scrolls. Back in Roman Times, mourners would fill small glass vials with tears and place them in burial tombs as symbols of love and respect. David talks about this in Psalm, reminding us that God cares about our sorrows also. He feels our pain and walks our journey with us.

This bottle will remind you that the Lord knows each tear you shed along your journey of healing; and He hears your heart's cry, and collects every tear you cry in the palm of His hand and saves them for you. I believe the Lord then takes our tears full of sorrows, trauma, heartache, and all which is held captive in our hearts, and collects them and then gives them back to us as blessings. Restoring our heart, healing our brokenness, and pouring out His love and joy for us are only a few of the blessings we will receive.

This bottle will speak to your heart each time you see it and remind you of the journey you took towards your new heart.

～ Masks For Healing ～

The purple mask stands for royalty. This masks represents the positive things Jesus says about us, believes us to be, and sees us as. We must see this also.

Black represents what is on the inside of our heart because of what we have been through: hurt, pain, shame, anger, depression, rejection and more. The word WALL is written in black on the forehead. You can't see it but it is there. It represents where it is hardened and darken from all the traumas built up and what is associated with the darkened pain.

The White mask represents all the negative things we hold off from our "make up mask." The white mask is decorated with makeup, all fixed up. Makeup represents all the things we do not show on the outside, which hides what is really under the makeup on the inside, and the negative part of ourselves we believe and never show. Our masks can be made up of many things. What is under your mask?

The more of the mask we take off and expose to others, the more freedom we will have. We gain this freedom by exposing what is under it and dealing with the painful issues in our heart. Healing begins as we are transparent. The more we expose the deeper the healing.

TAINTED LOVE	PURE LOVE
Lust	Seeks Purity
Immoral acts base of relationship	Gives Freely
Not given in return	Not Jealous
Shallow	Deep
Selfish	Selfless - Concerned for others
Cheating	Wellbeing of the other
Deceptive	Honest
Abusive	Gentle
Demeaning	Edifies
Controlling	Temperate
Callous	Compassionate
Tears down	Builds Up
Unforgiving	Forgiving
Judgmental	Non-Judgmental
Cruel	Kind
Fault Finding	Benefit of the Doubt
Impatient	Patient
Jealous	Trusting
Resist	Endures
Gives up	Never fails
Hopeless	Hopeful
Neglect	Believes
Evil thinking	Compassionate
Rude	Considerate
Prideful	Humble
Uncaring	Cares, heals
Insensitive	Sensitive to needs
Accusing	Pardon

*There are many others that can be mentioned. These are just a few.

⟨ What Is Forgiveness ⟩

Forgiveness does not change the past, but it does enlarge the future. –Paul Boese

Forgiveness is

Giving up the right to hurt someone who has hurt you.

Releasing the offender into God's hands for justice.

Picking up the tab – the person who hurt you will no

Longer owe you. The debt is canceled.

For your own Spiritual health.

A commandment from God.

Forgiveness is not

Trusting the person(s) who hurt you

Reconciliation

Forgetting, acquittal, or excusing

Necessarily a moment in time, but a process, a journey

Really Easy

For if you forgive men when they sin against you, your heavenly Father will also forgive you.
Matthew 6:14

"Do not take revenge my friends, but leave room for God's wrath, for it is written, "It's mine to avenge; I will repay," says the Lord. Romans 12:9

Scriptures about Babies Being in Heaven

The Bible talks about the "foreknown children" in heaven. This is simply saying that God knows all things before they even happen. It is the supernatural that only He contains; it is divine. God knows about our children who will be aborted beforehand, and is there waiting to receive their spirits at the time they are aborted. They are cared for in Heaven by God. They have real and eternal existence.

Your question may be, "If God knows we are going to have an abortion, since He is Omniscient, all knowing, then why did He allow us to get pregnant?" The answer is, we have a free will! God did not take that from us. He gives us life and our bodies were designed to give birth. He is the Creator. Our bodies were designed for this purpose. If we make a wrong choice, and it is time internally to be fertile, we will get pregnant. God's design, our choice!

Know that God loves our children we conceived and He is caring for them until are reunited with them.

2 Samuel 12:23	*"I will go to him, but he will not return to me."*
Ecclesiastes 12:7	*"The dust returns to the ground it came from and the spirit returns to God who gave it."*
Psalm 68:5	*"A father of the fatherless, a defender of widows, is God in His holy dwelling."*
1 Corinthians 15:40	*"There are also heavenly bodies and earthly bodies; but the splendor of the Heavenly bodies is one kind, and the splendor of the earthly bodies is another."*
Psalm 139:16	*"your eyes saw my unformed body, all the days ordained for me were written in Your book before one of them came to be."*
Mathew 18:10	*"See that you do not look down on one of these little ones. For I tell you that their angels in heaven always see the face of my Father in heaven."*
Psalm 22:10	*"From birth I was cast upon you, from my mother's womb you have been my God."*
Romans 7:9	*"Once I was alive apart from law; but when the commandment came sin sprang to life and I died."*

A Letter To My Daughter

My Dear Daughter,

I have been waiting for you to come to me with your burden that you have been carrying for so long. The excess weight of guilt, shame, embarrassment and fear that you have borne for such an extensive time is now about to be taken from you. I am overjoyed that you have finally called upon My name. I have waited patiently for you to come and let me embrace you in my loving arms, for I am your Abba Father; I am the one who created you and your child. I knew about you before I created the world, even before the beginning of time. I knit you inside of your mother's womb, I made you perfectly, and I knew the choices you would make. I knew the choices even before they formed in your own mind, and before you made that choice a reality. I also created your baby in a secret, dark place. Knowing all of this, I had a plan despite the choices and decisions you would make in your life. You now have asked me for forgiveness, which I freely bestow to you.

Please do not worry. Your baby has been in my care since that regrettable day. Your baby is safe in my arms, growing, and playing with many others. I love them all and their parents too! I know that your baby is looking forward to meeting you and spending all of eternity with both of us. You are My Beloved, My Princess and a daughter of the King! I love you so much that I sacrificed my own son's life so that you could have eternal life. Please accept this gift that includes the forgiveness of all your sins. I have taken your sin of abortion and thrown it into the deepest waters, never to resurface again. I now have work for you to do. Don't forget that I take all that Satan had intended for evil and turn it into good! Please learn from these compassionate women that have traveled this journey with you and join them in helping others who are hurting.

All My Love,

Abba Father

A Letter To My Son

Dear Beloved Son,

It has been such a long time that I have been waiting for you. Waiting for you to come to me with this burden you have carried for so long. You never suspected that the dysfunction in your life was directly connected to the guilt, shame, embarrassment and fear that follows an abortion. A new life awaits you. I am your Abba Father; I am the one who created you and your child. I knew about you even before I created the world, even before the beginning of time. I knit you inside of your mother's womb, I made you perfectly, and I knew the choices you would make. I knew the choices you would make even before they formed in your mind, and before that choice became a reality. I created your baby in secret, in the dark places. I felt your fear and your helplessness as you discussed what the mother of your baby was going to decide. You have asked me for your forgiveness, which I bestow upon you freely. My Son died on a cross for the purpose of saving man's soul if he would only accept this as truth and have faith in me. I placed my Son upon that Cross as FINAL payment for ALL of the sins of ALL of mankind, IF they accept my free gift of salvation.

Please do not worry. Your baby has been in my care since that regrettable day. Your baby is safe in my arms, growing, and playing with many others. I love them all and their parents too! I know that your baby is looking forward to meeting you and spending all of eternity with both of us. Have you taken me as the Lord and Savior of your life? I pray you do, because I long to be with you forever. I have work for you to do. Remember that I take all that Satan had intended for evil and turn it into good. I need you to tell your story. I need you to share your experience other young men that I send you and tell them how they can save their baby's life by simply telling the woman that he will support her in every way. I need you to support the Pro-Life movement. I need you to be the man I intended you to be. A man of integrity who will protect and provide for his family!

All My Love,

Abba Father

Brick by Brick Resources

1. BRICK BY BRICK Healing His Way A Devotional and Journal for Healing a Woman's Heart Hardback, Soft cover, EBook

2. BRICK BY BRICK Workbook Healing His Way A Journey & Study for Healing the Heart of Wounds from Abortion Soft Cover and EBook

3. BRICK BY BRICK Healing His Way A Devotional and Journal for Healing a Woman's Heart on CD

∽ Bibliography ∽

Covert, Keven. Brick *By Brick Healing His Way A Devotional and Journal for Healing A Woman's Heart,* Bloomington, IN: West Bow Press, Division of Thomas Nelson & Zondervan, 2015.

Hayford, Jack. *I'll Hold You in Heaven*, Ventura, CA: Regal Books, 1971

Lace, Millie. *Concepts of Recovery: The Journey.* Wayne, Arkansas: Concepts of Truth, Inc., 2011.

Layton, Patricia K. *Surrendering the Secret Healing for the Heartbreak of Abortion*, Grand Rapids, MI: Baker Books, 2014

The 5 Stages of Grief, Julie Axelrod, psychcentral.com

⟿ Acknowledgements ⟿

I want to first want to say thank you to my Lord and Savior, Jesus Christ who gave me the grace I needed to begin the Workbook to Brick By Brick Healing His Way, and the serene atmosphere and energy to bring it to completion. His patience through this entire process overwhelmed me. His desire to see the brokenhearted healed and walking in freedom is beyond words. His sacrifice gives us our victory.

To my incredible husband, who has supported me during this entire process and healing journey and who encouraged me hourly to "keep going". You once again came to my rescue with your patience concerning my IT issues. Your love and prayers were felt and sincerely appreciated. Thank you for creating the perfect atmosphere just as the Lord ordered. You are my earthly hero, the one I love and need by my side to go where the Lord is calling.

To Arleen Wong who has walked this journey with me from the very first day in 2013 when the Lord called me to write Brick By Brick Healing his Way. I remember you smiled and said, "Yes, I see you writing a healing guide let's get the book finished first." Three years later and the healing Workbook is completed. Thank you for believing in me and in what the Lord is going to do through this healing study. Thank you for being a part of this journey and being a co-author of the guide. Your friendship is invaluable. Also, thank you for your professional assistance in editing and rewording areas where needed.

Thank you to my three daughters, Kimberly Corter, Rebecca Wheatley, and Maranatha Covert for your continued prayers and support for the calling the Lord has placed on my life. You have supported me and encouraged me, reminding me of how needed this study will be. You are my beautiful blessings from the Lord.

Barbara Newton little did we know what the Lord had in His plans for us the summer of 2012 when we met. Look at us now, not only did we begin our healing journey together, but the Lord had plans and used us for His glory, to write a healing journey for women's hearts to be healed. Thank you so much for leading the post abortion healing ministry in South Florida. You're a special friend and it is a blessing to share this passion with you the Lord gave us both four years ago. Keep your passion and compassion.

Yadeline Franck, little did you know what the Lord had in store for you when you passed by my table fall of 2013. The Lord has since then delivered you from depression, took you on a journey of healing with Him, and put you over a Post Abortion Healing Ministry, and chose you to share in co-authoring this healing study for His glory. I'm so proud of all you persevered through. Keep that compassionate heart and continue to walk this journey with others to see them healed and walk in victory like you now do. Thank you for your obedience and picking up when the Lord moved me away. He's given you courage and making you stronger as the days to by. You're a special blessing. Yes, that's right, ALL for His Glory.

I am so proud of you Jennifer Perez for being bold and going where few will tread. Continue to take off your mask and share your story. Your transparency was the catalyst for others to have hope. Thank you so very much for being part of the healing guide for *BBB*. You are flowing in the Spirit sister! Your wisdom and gift of asking questions from God's heart will continue to touch others and be used for His Glory. Your passion to do God's will is evident and He will bless you for it. You're a special sister and blessing.

Thank you Diana Smith once again for going on an extension of my journey with *Brick By Brick*. You have been there from the very beginning. Your encouragement over this project and words of inspiration is what I needed when we would talk on the phone. Your patience was like gold, being used by the Lord as always. Good thing we don't pay for long distance phone calls any longer! Our friendship has grown and the miles have not kept us apart. You are a treasured blessing. Thank you for believing in me and having the vision for what the Lord wants to do with this project. You'll will always be a blessing and special friend in my life.

I want to say thank you to Libby Chapman, Cindy Levy and Mabel Reyes who told me the day of my book launch in 2015, this book needed to be turned into a healing study. I didn't dismiss it deep down, yet could not even "go there" at the time. The three of you praying over this project before it even came to be is from the Lord, I know. I could feel your prayers all the way up here in the mountains! Thank you for your continued encouragement, even with all the miles in between us. Miss you each!

Thank you Tina Krebs, my soul sister and newest sweet friend, for your passion and excitement you gave me when I needed it. Your encouraging words and prayers were timely. Your support in this project was amazing and I will be forever great full for how the Lord brought us together. He alone knows what is ahead. I wait in anticipation to see what is next for us. You are a blessing and inspiration to me. This healing ministry all of us are a part of is God's heart for the hurting. I'm blessed to be a part of it with you.

I want to thank Carol Thompson for taking time out of her busy schedule to read over this workbook and editing it for me. Having a second pair of eyes have been a blessing. Thank you so much for your assistance. Your time was a blessing and much appreciated!

Printed in the United States
By Bookmasters